Hello
Darkness

Hello
Darkness

My doctor said,
"Son, you will be
blind tomorrow."

Sanford D.
Greenberg

Post Hill
PRESS

A POST HILL PRESS BOOK

Hello Darkness:
My doctor said, "Son, you will be blind tomorrow."
© 2022 by Sanford D. Greenberg
All Rights Reserved

ISBN: 978-1-63758-274-9
ISBN (eBook): 978-1-63758-275-6

Cover design by Jason Heuer
Interior design and composition by Greg Johnson, Textbook Perfect

This is a work of nonfiction. All people, locations, events, and situations are portrayed to the best of the author's memory.

Post Hill Press
New York • Nashville
posthillpress.com

Published in the United States of America
Distributed by Simon and Schuster
1 2 3 4 5 6 7 8 9 10

Honestly, it wasn't just me!
They really did dress kids
like this way back in the day.

From the first page to the last, I was captivated by Sandy's bright mind, ready wit, and indomitable spirit.

—**Ruth Bader Ginsburg**
Associate Justice of the
United States Supreme Court,
1993–2020

Sandy is my gold standard of decency.
I try to be his cantor, the tallis that embraces him.

—**Art Garfunkel**
recording artist,
winner of eight Grammy awards,
inductee of the Rock and Roll Hall of Fame

How devastating it would have been to be told at such a young age that you would never see again. What willpower it would have taken to paddle upstream against such a strong current. And how encouraging it is to know it can be done, because Sanford Greenberg did it—with a little help from his friends, but we all need that.

—**Margaret Atwood**
author of *The Handmaid's Tale* and other novels,
two-time winner of the Booker Prize

For Sue,
the one who has always been there

the dark beyond dark
the door to all beginnings

—LAO-TZU, *Tao Te Ching*

Author's Note

You would think that a book about a young man going blind would be very sad. I went blind at age nineteen, and, yes, there were some awfully hard times. But my story is more than a tragedy. In fact, it's not really a tragedy at all.

I think of my life in three acts, like a play. In Act One, I was young boy, raised by poor but loving parents just after World War II.

In Act Two, I went to a great college and had a promising future ahead of me. Then—*wham!*—I got a disease that left me blind.

In Act Three—well, you'll just have to read this book to find out what happened. Along the way there are tears and laughter, painful moments and wonderful times.

When you go blind after nineteen years, you remember a lot of what the world looked like. You remember all kinds of things. After I went blind, my memory became like muscle that grew stronger every day. I remember so much that I just had to write it down. What follows are some of the low and high points of my life.

My Father

Have you ever had a dream that you dreamed many times? Not every night, but maybe a few times a year? This happened to me a long time ago when I was a boy. The dream was not a happy one, but it's important to my story, so I'll tell it to you.

In the dream it is a sunny late-summer day at Crystal Beach in Canada, just west of Buffalo, New York. A tall, handsome father in a bathing suit is carrying his five-year-old son on his back about twenty yards from shore out into Lake Erie. Both are laughing as the father runs through the waves. The father playfully lowers himself and his son into the lake, and as the water slaps at the child's bathing suit, the boy begins to tremble and laugh. Danger excites him; he has never been out in the water before. But in his father's arms he is safe.

Suddenly, the father, still holding the boy, turns and pushes through the water toward the shore. The boy is surprised and at first amused. At the shoreline, the father hesitates for an instant. Then he slams facedown on the hard, wet sand, forcing the boy's face into it. The boy rolls his father over and sees his glazed and vacant eyes. The father is dead. The boy sits and stares blankly.

The reason for this dream is clear. In 1946, I went on my first trip to the beach. Later that same year, my father died. The beach trip was an important early memory, but soon after, a bigger event happened—the death of my father—and my dream mixed the two together.

My father, Albert Greenberg, was a tailor who had to work long, hard hours to provide for his family. He had very little time left over to spend with his children. I admired him, but since he died when I was five years old, I don't have many memories of him.

I remember his last morning. My little brother, Joel, and I walked him to the streetcar stop and waved goodbye as he left for work. We found out later that at lunchtime he walked to the corner pharmacy, where he collapsed and died. I never knew exactly what he died of. Probably a heart attack from years of stress. Albert grew up in a small village in Poland, in Eastern Europe. He was Jewish, and this was a very bad time to be Jewish in Eastern Europe. Because times were hard, people often took their frustrations out on Jewish people, smashing up their shops and homes and making life miserable for them.

In 1934, Albert, as a young man, moved with his family to Cologne, Germany. Cologne was a city of culture and refinement, so they thought it would be a better place for a Jewish family. Boy were they wrong!

The Nazis had just come to power in Germany. They began rounding up Jewish people and sending them to concentration camps, where they were forced to work as slaves. Many died or were killed. Albert and a group of his family and friends made it out of Germany just in time. They spent many months wandering about Europe, walking from place to place, knocking on doors, looking for shelter. They were lucky to find people kind and brave enough to help them. Finally, in 1939, almost two years before I was born, they made it to Paris, France. But the Nazis were not far behind. My father and the others migrated to the United States just before the Nazis invaded France.

He settled in Buffalo, New York, where he was free to earn a living without being persecuted for being Jewish. But he never lost the habit of looking over his shoulder for danger. The stress finally caught up to him that day inside the pharmacy in Buffalo.

That evening, his coffin lay in the center of our living room in Buffalo, draped with a black velvet cloth embroidered with a Star of David. I thought the cloth was keeping him warm. Remember, I was five years old. I knew he was dead, but I didn't really know what that meant. Candles representing the divine spark in the human body burned in red glass containers. I touched the coffin with my fingers, playing on it as if it were a piano. I sat under it like a good boy. I fiddled with the loose stitching of the cloth that hung below the bottom of the casket. I knew it was a terrible occasion, though I did not know precisely why. I was frightened and confused.

Then came the burial. It was a bleak, gray day. Wind swept across the cemetery. We huddled together like peasants. I stood among the adults at the burial site, unable to make sense of the silent scene—as perhaps no five-year-old could. The mounds of dirt surrounded a large rectangular hole in the earth. The coffin rested to one side. Amid the sobs of those gathered around me, the rabbi began chanting a prayer. We put my father in the ground. The coffin was lowered on worn leather straps until it was nearly at the bottom. There were only a few inches between him and the cold ground, but in my mind he wasn't quite buried yet. And so that meant maybe he wasn't really dead. We could open the coffin. He could come out. Climb out of the hole, come home, and shower. Have lunch, live a good, long life.

Then the straps suspending the coffin were unhooked and whipped out. Next came something worse. Those who volunteered were each handed a shovel, and they took turns throwing soil onto the coffin. I know now that this act is thought by Jewish people to be a *mitzvah*, a good deed. But at the time it felt the opposite. I had a strong urge to jump into the hole to rescue my father. Yet I stood motionless as each new shovelful of earth landed on top of the coffin with a thud.

My father's death changed my world. I was now the man of the family—something I recall comprehending even at that young age. I felt responsible for my mother and my little brother and sister. My father had been the head of the family, but now we were down to four and I was the oldest male.

I was sad, but I also remember feeling an uncomfortable sense of freedom. I know that sounds strange, but it's true. I'm old now, so I want to tell you only what I know to be true. I clearly recall feeling free. Not triumphant or joyful, just free in a new way. Yes, there was a wretched feeling of loss that has stayed vivid in my memory, but blessedly, there was a new feeling opening up in me. It was a little scary, because I didn't really understand it. I realized after my father's death that I no longer had the same limits and restraints. That realization was an "epiphany." I've had many epiphanies in my life, times when things suddenly come together in my mind in a new way. They're kind of thrilling. I'll tell you about some others later on.

Anyway, some years later I read a passage in the Bible, in which God commanded Abraham to "go forth." He also told Abraham to leave everything behind. I remembered comparing Abraham's situation with mine. Abraham had a specific destination. I didn't. I had to stay in Buffalo and grow up and be a good son and help take care of my brother and sister. After that, I didn't know where I was supposed to go, but I knew one thing—I wouldn't have to leave everything behind. My family and friends would always be there with me.

I'm on the bottom left, with
my younger brother Joel and
my parents, Sarah and Albert.
My dad died when I was five,
leaving Mom with $54 to
begin raising Joel, me, and our
younger sister Ruthie.

This knowledge has made all the difference in my survival. When I was a young man in college, I went blind. That's a lot of what this story is about. But not completely. What happened *after* I went blind is much more important. But before I get into that, I need to tell you about the things that happened between my father's death and my loss of sight. The reason I told you about my father's death is that it taught me something big: if I could handle that, I could handle just about anything.

Mother

My mother, Sarah, was a quiet person, but she loved to dance. She liked coffee more than tea. She met my father on a street in Buffalo, and according to her, it was love at first sight. I like to imagine that right after they met, he couldn't stop thinking about her—that he went back to his tailor shop and, while sizing up a man's sleeve, pricked himself with a pin. Marriage followed not long afterward.

They went on vacation to Florida once. They sat by the pool, held hands for a moment, found the light too bright, and left. They went out to dinner. She thought about her girl-friends. She thought about her children, the neighborhood, wanting us to be safe. She knew where we were because we were with *her* mother, having a ball.

Mother would hold my hand. She held my hand as we crossed the railroad tracks, and she would hold me back as the Erie-Lackawanna train roared past. She held my hand when we went to synagogue. She held my hand whenever we crossed the street, went on trips to see Niagara Falls, went to an apple orchard, went to Crystal Beach. Her hand had seen work—a layer of tough skin covered the softer skin, mostly from her later work assembling airplane parts at the factory.

My father's death left my mother with a total of fifty-four dollars to support herself, me, Joel, and Ruthie, our six-month-old sister. In desperation, she approached the Jewish Federation for assistance and was told that it would be forthcoming—but only if she agreed to place her children in three separate orphanages. The notion revolted her. She made up her mind never to permit any institution or individual to break up her family. To support us, she became a saleslady at Sattler's department store and then at the Broadway Market, both in Buffalo.

With fifty-four dollars to begin our new life, Mother could do the following:

She could buy us food and cook a dinner: a beef brisket, sweet gravy, and potatoes. She made sure her children ate before she did.

She could take us to the movies, but not often.

She could buy four sticks of gum—pink and sweet.

She could take us to Crystal Beach—the public area only.

She could teach manners, even elegance, in the face of poverty.

She could put on three sets of boots, coats, mittens, and scarves and see us off to school in the morning.

She could give us a kiss on the cheek.

She could withhold her own fear and anxiety.

She could absorb *our* fear and anxiety and pain. Almost all.

She could tuck us into bed at night.

She could shed light. At least it sometimes seemed that way to us. She was like a bright spot on a satellite photograph of Earth at night.

* * *

In the 1940s until well through elementary school, I lived in a kind of *shtetl*, a bleak neighborhood in a poor section on Buffalo's East Side. In the early years of my childhood, after my father's death, my mother had to shuffle us from one boardinghouse to another. We knew that we might not be staying at any place for very long. "Don't disturb the landlord" was the evening watchword. It was practically the eleventh Commandment, along with, "Be seen and not heard."

We finally rented a house, at 163 Butler Avenue on the East Side. But maybe because I was the oldest child, I continued to be worried about our uncertain living situation. Somehow that worry turned into a fear of blindness and cancer. The first poem I wrote was about the horror of both these dread afflictions. I don't remember the poem, just the subject.

I remember standing hand in hand with my mother at the local ritual slaughterhouse while she ordered a kosher chicken, our Friday night dinner. The *shochet* (butcher) would chop its head off right in front of us. The blood squirting from its neck would run down a trough, and the chicken's head would lie on the side, staring up at you as if to say, "Can this be? Is this possible?"

One time, the sight was more than I could take. Before I could be sick, my mother dragged me out into the fresh air, where I promptly stumbled over a blind beggar. The sight of him was almost as bad as the headless chicken. He was sitting cross-legged on the sidewalk. He was lean and lanky, hunched over in torn and soiled clothes, which were two sizes too big. His eyes were unfocused and milky, with small black spots. His teeth were decayed and misshapen. He held a metal cup. After that, he became a regular visitor to my dreams.

The park near our home was dangerous. Thugs lurked there even in the daytime, and they would often beat us up just for the fun of it. For amusement, we would go behind our house to play. It wasn't really a yard, just a small area. My great-uncle Abraham, who owned the house, worked back there, stripping metal from bedposts over an anvil—a heavy iron block. All day long, that old white-haired man would hunch over the anvil, clanking away. His weary horse stood in its tiny stable in the rear, likely grateful for the break from hauling a heavy junk cart. Joel and I had to be careful not to get in Uncle Abraham's way or he would growl at us in Yiddish.

You could hear conversations in the upper rooms of all the homes in the neighborhood—sometimes they were arguments, and sometimes they were loud. Mostly, though, the neighbors tended to be quiet. Many of them, like my father, had escaped from the horrors of the Nazis, and they were guarded in their speech. Although I was young then and did not know why they were so quiet, I got a sense of it.

Despite all that, there were good times as well. My brother and I would play football or baseball in the middle of the street until early evening. It was hot and muggy and we loved it. You could hear the bugs whirring up near the streetlamps. The old neighborhood women would be in their housedresses, watching us from their porches. Will Ludwig, an old blind man, would stand and "watch" us also. No one knew what he did or where he came from. He just stood there in his white T-shirt and gray slacks hiked up on his hips. He was creepy but harmless, like a friendly ghost. If he wasn't there, you wouldn't notice his absence. He would always stand on the same spot, arms folded, as though he were a referee. Somehow, his presence softened the harshness of the light from the streetlamps. There came a time when we realized that he no longer appeared in the evenings. I don't know what became of him.

I have some other good memories of those early years. There was always the wonderful feeling when I would get to spend the day with my grandmother, for instance. I remember the soothing smell of my mother's cold cream and the scent of her perfume, the look and feel of her worn dress, the swish of her house slippers against the wood floors, the smoothness of her voice, the sounds of her sipping coffee, the clink of the saucer, and the pattern on the window drapes in her room. I remember the joy of coming in from a frigid winter walk with my little brother, entering an envelope of warmth and calm, and singing "Shalom Aleichem" to welcome the Sabbath on Friday evenings. I remember reciting the blessings, sitting down, and beginning to eat. These were the little things that underpinned my world.

* * *

AFTER ABOUT FIVE YEARS of living in poverty, my mother married Uncle Carl, my father's brother. Carl was a junk dealer—that is, he bought and sold scrap metal, rags, old newspapers, cardboard, glass, pieces of wood, and other items people wanted to get rid of. He was like an early recycler. Although the way Carl earned a living was far from glamorous, he was at least able to buy us a home. It had a yard, a real living room, and even a television set. It was hardly a mansion, but it didn't need to be. From the kitchen window, we could see the sun rise. And from the picture window in the den, we could watch it set. Many times, I would sit contentedly in *my* house, *our* house, watching the sun set. I also watched it in the nearby park with my little brother, while playing basketball, as the days would wear on into evening. Life sure was better in this neighborhood.

After our family moved to the new house—182 Saranac Avenue in north Buffalo—and I was placed in a new school, the contrast with our old life was striking. I now had a chance to start fresh, to pretend that all that had happened before had not happened. Things were beginning to look good. My family's optimism matched that of the whole country. This was in the early 1950s, not long after World War II, when American families were feeling prosperous and hopeful about the future. It was as if I, my family, and my country had together emerged from a dark tunnel into the light.

3

Grandma

My mother also supported my beloved grandmother, Pauline Fox. We called her Grandma, or *Bub*. Born in Poland, Grandma was a survivor of Jewish ghettos, poverty, and pogroms (massacres of defenseless people). When she was eight years old, she suffered a bizarre accident that resulted in the loss of her left eye. While she was babysitting, a spring popped out of a crib and hit her in the eye. She never spoke of her partial blindness, but on late evenings Joel and I would see her remove her glass eye and place it in her dresser. Sometimes we would secretly open the drawer, shivering at that spooky eye staring back at us.

Grandma escaped the pogroms by moving to London, England, where she operated a candy store in a crummy part of town. Shortly after arriving in Buffalo in the early 1900s, she fell ill and remained in poor health for the rest of her life. Her illness may have had to do with her exhaustion, like my father's, from escaping death in Europe. Yet somehow she toughed it out, supported herself in England, learned a new language, and made her way across the Atlantic Ocean to the United States. It was all a huge endeavor for a rather slight woman from a tiny town in Eastern Europe.

But within Grandma, the spark of life still burned. She passed that spark on to her grandchildren. Besides her endurance and wisdom, the main things that kept her going were her family and the weekly Sabbath. She and my mother used to cover their eyes when they lit the Sabbath candles. We do the same today. It is a ritual, and it is as if we light the same set of candles, candles that join us with generations across great distances and many years. So long as I live, I will think of Grandma with love and gratitude.

She lived with us, and we thought of her as a second mother. She was like the wise elder of our tribe. We received doses of advice and wisdom from her, more than we sought. It was possible to believe she had the ability to do magic. Her dignity led us to this belief. To sit with her was good fortune. Her hands were solid—they had experienced so much. In them there was great knowledge. We would be lucky if one day our hands would know half as much. It was almost too much to be close to her, as if you might not be worthy of it. We were around her like excited chicks around a hen— always at her feet. When I grew taller than her, it was still the same way. To hug her was to be blessed; you left feeling stronger. Her age was the source of her strength, her false eye the source of mysterious power.

Grandma would sit on the porch watching us playing ball in the street. She never had to say anything to us, never had to shout, "Good hit" or "Good catch." It would have demeaned her. When she supervised, she was beyond language. When she did speak, it was in Yiddish. We listened to every word as if no one else in our lives would ever say something like it again, as if what she told us was how we ought to be. She was like an angel that way.

I remember the feel of her cotton housedress against my face as I hugged her. Her papery hands on my neck. Her lips on the top of my head. The layer of white sand she kept in the bottom of my old baby dresser—brought back by friends, at her request, from trips to the Holy Land in Israel. Her black rocking chair on the left side of the porch. The solitude of listening to the radio with her on Wednesday and Thursday evenings. Those times lasted past childhood, into my adulthood.

Here I am, barely born, with
my Grandmother Pauline.
She survived Jewish ghettos,
poverty, and pogroms to get
to America. Grandma spoke
only in Yiddish, and we
listened to her every word
like our lives depended on it.

4

A Second Father

Carl Greenberg was a relatively short man, but he possessed a powerful body. His enormous physical strength and firm character came in handy when he made a difficult escape from Nazi Germany in the mid-1930s. He and a handful of friends and family left in the middle of the night, crossed the Rhine River, and eventually went on to England and the United States. From there he worked to save the rest of his family, including my father, Albert. The details are sketchy, because Carl was not one for talking about those times. His strength also helped him thrive in Buffalo's rough-and-tumble scrap metal and junk business. One day an employee with a bad temper threw a brick at him, catching him in one eye. As with my grandmother, it was replaced by a glass eye.

During the summers, when I was out of school, I worked in Carl's junkyard. Wading around in piles of junk was not as fun as it might sound. It was man's work, and I was not yet a man. Much of my job consisted of winding metal wire around bales of rags and locking it in place so the bales could be weighed and transported. The rags stank like wet dust. The bales weighed several hundred pounds and were hard to handle. The metal would scrape and infect my arms, and the locking mechanisms would pinch my fingers and knuckles. We used a mechanical lift to get the bales onto the scale and then to push them into the bed of the truck. The bales would sit on the truck bed like giant eggs in a carton. The junk shop collected and sold various metals as well as rags. Sometimes we would collect brass bed frames. Using an old hammer and a screwdriver, we would split and peel the brass off the supports in order to sell it. We sold other metals, too, although for a lot less money.

Carl kept a pile of receipts on a thin metal spindle. His script was European-style—blunt and thick, as if his hands were unsuited for the act of writing. His handwriting was nearly illegible. Black ink was dug like canals into the paper. Carl did not talk much at his shop; he gave orders in quick bursts. He would tell me where to go or what to do. There was no discussion. In summer the scrap yard was roasting hot and foul-smelling; the only shade came from a large, rumpled sheet-metal roof that stood over one end of the yard. The rest was open. The smell of copper and corroded metal would get in your nose and your lungs and sting your eyes. And the sun's reflection off the metal was like a laser. I had to be careful or the sharp edges would split the skin of my shins like paper.

Two men worked for Carl at the junk shop. Arthur was a giant. He could lift metal furniture all by himself and launch it into the dumpster. I thought him capable of terrible things. He wasn't violent (that I saw), but I always kept my distance. Years later, rushing through an airport, I accidentally knocked, straight-on, into the famous heavyweight boxer Muhammad Ali. And that is what Arthur was like—a huge block of a man.

The other man, Donald, was much smaller, wiry and muscular. He was really the only source of conversation I had in the junkyard. He told me once that he lived in a boardinghouse in what I knew to be the poorest section of Buffalo. He paid twenty-five cents a night to stay there. At lunch break, we would sit outside the junkyard on the side-walk curb, his glasses low on his nose, a floppy brown hat on his head. The street would be quiet in the heat. He would drink sweet muscatel wine but eat nothing. I would eat the tuna-fish sandwich that my mother usually packed for me. It was embarrassing. What must he have thought of someone whose mommy packed his lunch? I sometimes offered him half of my sandwich, but he always declined.

For a treat, Carl would give me a nickel to go across the street to the small convenience store and buy a grape soda. It was a very big deal for me. The man who worked there knew

After five years of living
in rough conditions, my
mother married Carl, a junkyard
dealer, and we moved into his
sunny house on a tree-lined
street. I was thrilled to have
a second dad.

how big a deal it was and was always happy to see me. Maybe he was just happy that I was so happy.

* * *

I WOULD OFTEN WONDER whether Carl was ashamed of his line of work. I was, a little, even though I thought of him as a good father, not just a stepfather. I became president of my class at Bennett High School, and I had a girlfriend. It was embarrassing explaining to her that my father ran a junk shop. Her father sold clothing, a respectable job for a family man. Sometimes I was proud of my summer job and Carl's business—after all, there's nothing wrong with good old-fashioned hands-on work. But for the most part I was ashamed. It was sometime later that I realized my shame was much more shameful than the work.

I might have ended up in the junk business myself had not certain things intervened.

5

Sue

When I was in sixth grade, I met a girl who changed my entire life. I didn't really "meet" her. We were in the same class, and I noticed her. I don't think she noticed me at all, at least not for some time.

While I retain many vivid visual memories from the days on Saranac Avenue in Buffalo, none is more vivid than the day when I first noticed Sue Roseno. I had never seen someone so beautiful and so graceful in my life. As she began to answer the teacher, I was dumbstruck by her features and her voice. I just stared.

I watched her in class. I watched her walk down the hallway with her friends. I watched her on her bike, following her from behind. Like the Lady of the Lake of Arthurian legend, she rose up out of the water on a day when I was lost in the forest and said, "Now, listen."

She wanted nothing to do with me. She was tall and had brown hair, an arched back, and a double-jointed thumb, which fascinated me. She would not say hello to me in class or in the hallways. I would think, "Please say hello to me. I can't be the first to do it. I'm scared. But if you do it, then I can say hello back, and maybe by then I'll have thought of some questions: Where do you live? What sports do you like? Do you even like sports?" But she said nothing to me, which was the most reasonable thing in the world because I never said anything to her.

The first time our teacher said Sue's name—*Sue*—I was captivated by the sound of the word. But nothing compared to the image of her walking to the front of the class to give a report on—something. I don't remember what. Who cared? All I could remember, and it would haunt me later, was the swoop of the small of her back, her shoulders, the sweater she was wearing, as if she were a woman emerging from the body of a young girl, and though I was tall, and myself becoming a young man, I could not believe it was happening. I could not get the thought of her out of my mind.

In time, I took a small step toward getting to know her. In eighth grade, we were the two finalists in the school spelling bee sponsored by the *Buffalo Evening News*, one of the two leading Buffalo newspapers. Sue, up first, was asked to spell "silhouette." She misspelled it!

Then it was my turn. I might have flubbed it on purpose so that she could win, but I spelled it correctly. Beating her was a risky way to get her to notice me. I figured that by winning the spelling bee I would at least have her respect.

* * *

IN HIGH SCHOOL I became involved in all kinds of activities. I joined a number of clubs; I played ice hockey and played on the baseball and basketball teams. I took trumpet lessons because I thought playing the trumpet was cool. Although my family had to suffer through my practicing, I was becoming good, or thought I was. Anyway, I was good enough for the high school orchestra. I loved making music; it made me feel terrific. Music hides certain things and reveals certain other things. I was able to use both the effort and the sound to cover over the memory of the terrible silence of my previous life in the old neighborhood.

I played the trumpet not only to break the silence but also to cover up my lack of a father. A young boy may not precisely comprehend the deeper importance of that hole in his life, but he becomes aware of it when he sees other boys with their dads, playing ball or going for walks. He experiences it when the other boys have a new bike to show off, or a new baseball mitt, or a pack of baseball cards. I could never say, "My dad got me this, check it out." I was not even able to say that my mother got me this or that, because she couldn't afford to buy anything as unimportant as a baseball glove. What I did receive was always a hand-me-down.

My Bar Mitzvah portrait,
age 13, a day I will always
remember. Even before I
went blind, my Jewish faith
sustained me through many
troubled times.

To say that things were much better in my new life doesn't mean everything was miserable before. It also doesn't mean that things were perfect now. Carl's junk business was not going to make us rich. If anything, he was just barely making a go of it, and sometimes he was losing ground. I became more aware of this during high school. But I knew that, at least for the time being, we were doing okay in our new house and neighborhood. I had other concerns.

* * *

I WAS DETERMINED TO get Sue interested in me. It was not until my second year in high school that she began to pay attention to me. Up until this time I hadn't figured out a way to make a good impression. Saying "hi" in the hallway was a start, but it led nowhere. Then, in sophomore year, I decided to invite her to my fraternity's annual Cancer Charity Ball. It was kind of a grown-up thing for a sixteen-year-old kid to do—go to a charity ball, let alone invite a date. But she accepted!

I didn't have a tuxedo and couldn't afford to rent one, so I put on the only suit I owned. It was navy blue, and I figured that was close enough to a black tuxedo. I drove to her house to pick her up, knocked nervously on the turquoise front door (my heart pounding), and was greeted by a stunning young woman. I froze. I wish I could tell you what she was wearing, but all I can remember was standing there staring at a woman dressed for a fancy evening event who bore a startling resemblance to a girl known as Sue, a serious girl from

What could be better than
driving for the first time?
(Note the argyle socks!)
Three years later, with failing
vision, I careened into two
parked cars on a snowy street
and never drove again.

school. This beaming girl, her hair done in the latest style, couldn't be Sue. And yet she was. Anyway, she sounded like Sue. Although my eyes were fixed on her, she appeared not to notice that I was staring. She took my hand and welcomed me into her home, introducing me to her parents, who greeted me warmly.

Sue and I went to the ball and had a wonderful time dancing and pretending to be about twice as old as we were. And that was the beginning. Sometimes we would go out to an apple orchard in the countryside on fall weekends. We would pick up apples that had fallen to the ground and then walk between the trees, holding hands. Then we might stop and kiss for a little while. In the evenings we would often go on a date with another couple. We might get something to eat or go to a movie, but mostly we would talk...and talk. I usually had a great deal to say; there was lots of sorting out to do, deciding who in our circle belonged to what group, trying to understand where and how we fit in.

I was a busy boy in high school, and Sue was a busy girl. She loved to talk on the phone. I preferred talking in person. We both enjoyed sitting in the car on the weekends doing what teenagers did—kissing, yes, but also imagining a future together, happy in knowing who we were. High school went by like that—always so much to do and as much fun as it should be, for me at any rate. It seemed to me then that all my really hard times were in my rearview mirror. The future looked amazing—filled with challenges that I would choose and limitless possibilities.

The crowning moment of my growing up in Buffalo, the one etched most clearly in my memory, was my high school graduation. When the musical introduction, Beethoven's "Ode to Joy," concluded, the audience buzzed with anticipation. I stood just outside the auditorium, nervous, my black graduation gown almost touching the floor, my mortarboard tilted slightly. My seventeen years of life seemed to have led to this one instant. As class president, I entered the auditorium at the head of my classmates. After a few steps, I stopped. The eyes of the audience were on me. I waited, looked around the room, and smiled, catching my mother's eye. I sensed her enormous pride and knew at that moment that I had it all.

Here is the entry for Sanford D. Greenberg in the 1958 yearbook of Bennett High School, Buffalo, New York:

> President of the senior class; president of the student council; president of the Buffalo Inter-High School Student Council; representative of the Empire Boy's State; associate editor of the school yearbook; chief consul of the senior class; member of the Bennett High School Hall of Fame; member of the Legion of Honor, Key Club, French Honorary Society, cross-country team, and track team. Prom king.

I include that entry here for two reasons. I wanted to show you how busy I was. If it seems a little like bragging, well, it's my story and I want to tell it right. Why hide the stuff I did? The other reason is that while I was on top of the world then, I would soon be so deep on the bottom that my high school self could not have imagined it. Life is like that sometimes. Everything is going great, and then—*wham!*—something comes along and sets you farther back than you ever were. There is a line from Proverbs in the Bible that says, "Pride goeth before destruction." I was pretty proud of myself, but even if I hadn't been, I was in for a big tumble. What was coming was coming.

My past seven years had been filled with sunlight, love, friendships, happiness, and (to my mind) enormous accomplishments. I was about to enter Columbia University in New York City, and after that, even more exciting possibilities would without a doubt open up for me.

Before I left home for my freshman year at college, Sue and I agreed that we should date other people, at least while I was away in the city and she was at college in Buffalo. This was supposedly to allow us to see whether our love would stand the test of time. Maybe that sounds crazy. Go out with other people to make sure you really love your girlfriend or boyfriend? But that's what young people did, and still do. We thought it was very wise and sophisticated. As it would turn out, our love had to stand a much rougher test than the passage of time and a distance of four hundred miles.

I fell for Sue in the sixth grade,
finally got up the nerve to talk
with her a few years later, and
took her to the prom our senior year.

6

College

After a summer of anticipation, I found myself at last on an airplane headed to New York City to begin my college years. Late in the evening that same day, holding my one suitcase (it was green), I arrived at Broadway and 116th Street to stand before the massive iron gates leading to Columbia University's main pedestrian artery, College Walk. The gates were open inward, as if in welcome, the walkway framed by two magnificent libraries. I understood that this was one of the great moments of my life. In a golden haze, I entered.

I had planned to study Judaism and its traditions, but I soon changed my focus to government studies and international affairs. Columbia was chock-full of important professors, many of whom had written big, impressive books. I was soon under their spell, dazzled by how much they knew. They were like sorcerers in their fields, and I was a willing apprentice.

Each morning I walked from my dormitory, New Hall, past a big bronze statue of Alexander Hamilton, one of my favorite Founding Fathers. (Yes, the same Alexander Hamilton who inspired Lin-Manuel Miranda's super-hit musical *Hamilton*!) Hamilton had been a Columbia student way back in 1774. Sometimes I would just stand before his statue in awe. I was kind of a nerd that way. But I also felt I had something in common with the great man. Jewish people have always felt themselves to be "strangers in a strange land." Hamilton wasn't Jewish, but he was an outsider, having come to America from the Caribbean islands. As a foreigner, he knew that he would have to work extra hard in order for people to take him seriously. His burning desire to achieve, achieve, achieve was an inspiration for me in my early college days and would be even more so after I suffered a serious setback.

One sunny day in April 1959, I met with one of my professors in his Hamilton Hall office. He was dressed casually in a brown tweed sport coat and an open-collared plaid shirt. He had a deep divot in his chin, which I couldn't help but notice as he sat facing me on a swivel chair. Details like that were important because they made these men and women, who were like gods to me, into real human beings. I knew that this professor rode a motorcycle to his office every day and that he had written some important books. After he had talked for a while, I dared to ask him, "Sir, how does one write a great book?"

He instantly responded, "Write one thousand words each and every day—it's that simple."

So there were practical answers to some of the secrets of these magicians. The next day I was back in Hamilton Hall talking to a fellow Buffalonian. He also happened to be a Pulitzer Prize–winning historian whose opinion on American politics was valued by many people around the country. But even though he was a big shot, he was also a Columbia professor. Which meant that I could go talk to him in his office. This was a great privilege for a young man like me.

This professor was recognized on campus for his bow tie and his friendly manner. We talked for a while on important topics of the day—well, mostly he talked and I listened. I was waiting for the right moment to ask him one burning question. Finally, I blurted out, "Professor, how do you become president of the United States?"

(I was asking a lot of questions like that back then!)

The professor pulled back and eyed me carefully. He did not say, "Young man, is it your ambition to become the president?" If he had, I'm not sure what I would have said, probably something like, "No, but maybe governor of New York." I did have a lot of ambition, which is not a bad thing for a young person to have, as long as there's a good reason for the ambition. I thought I was smart and talented, and I wanted to do something good for the country, so politics seemed like a reasonable direction to take.

The great professor considered my question, placed his elbow on his desk, and then tilted his head and rested his cheek on his fist. For the longest time he said nothing. I shifted nervously in my chair, hoping that there would soon be a response of some sort, but short of ridicule. Then he said, "Put yourself in the stream of history."

I left his office wondering what he meant. But I knew that, one way or another, I was going to stay involved in politics for the rest of my life, because this country had been the salvation of my family. Some of my family members died at the hands of the Nazis; without the United States, many more would have.

I was also interested in the arts, and my art history professor trained us to take a blank sheet with a small hole in the middle and move it so that we could follow individual lines or sections in various great drawings. Doing this line by line or section by section, we learned to be able to put together each drawing from its parts by memory. This strange ability turned out to be one of the saving graces of my later life, helping me reconstitute mental images of many works of art.

In yet another class, physics, there was a cannonball suspended from a long black chain at the front of the classroom. On the first day, the professor stood patiently until everyone was seated. He then grabbed the cannonball, walked it to the side of the room, climbed onto a chair, held the ball a millimeter in front of his nose, and then let it go. It swung to the other side of the room. As the ball swung back toward him, we gasped, expecting it to smash into his face. Maybe you already know that a pendulum will return exactly to where it started (minus a little bit because of friction), but we college students did not. The ball came very close to smacking his nose, but it didn't. We liked this professor and his demonstrations quite a bit, and if you ever have a chance to take a physics class, I hope you will, for you will learn a lot about how the whole universe works.

My physics professor's name was Leon Lederman, and he became famous for discovering two particles smaller than an atom. They are called muon neutrinos and bottom quarks. Don't ask me what they are, because even though I took his class, I don't know. Perhaps you are picturing a professor hovering over a microscope looking for something very, very tiny. I don't blame you; I did the same thing. But they're invisible. Professor Lederman and two of his colleagues discovered the particles by using a lot of very complicated math, some experiments with fancy laboratory equipment, and their imagination. When he would tell us about his work, he became so excited that he talked faster than the speed of sound. That's an exaggeration, but he did talk so fast we sometimes wondered if he was a little wacky. My friends and I didn't realize how famous he was in the field of particle physics; he later won a Nobel Prize. And thanks to him, I had a solid foundation in science that helped when I started a technology business.

All these teachers were carrying on the work of the many great thinkers who came before them. And they passed along

When I woke up blind in a
hospital bed in February 1961,
I thought my college days were
over. Instead, fifteen months
later I graduated from Columbia
University as president of my class.

their knowledge to us, for which I will be forever grateful. They helped set my sights high, bolstered my self-esteem, and firmed up my determination to be as much like them as I could. I didn't see myself going into teaching, but I knew I wanted to carry their wisdom and learning with me wherever I went. Without those teachers and their world of ideas, I would have had a very hard time when it came to living without sight.

7

Shadow Education

Columbia University is located on the north end of the island of Manhattan, and Manhattan is the heart of the exciting, bustling city of New York. In other words, I was going to college in one of the greatest cities in the world. For a boy from Buffalo, New York City was a magnificent and magical peach, its sweet riches begging to be tasted. I couldn't wait to get started.

With one or two of my favorite classmates, I began exploring the various neighborhoods, among them Greenwich Village, Chinatown, Little Italy, and Harlem. Each had its own distinct character and flavor, its own look, its own sounds and smells. There were cafés and clubs and music and street fairs, so many things to dazzle a kid with no big-city experience. The only problem was deciding where to go next. I loved the jazz, folk, and rock music in Greenwich Village, but there was also the delicious food in Little Italy. And everywhere there were museums and art galleries and secondhand bookstores. Did I mention concerts and plays? We wanted to see and do it all. Four years didn't seem like long enough. As it turned out, I would have only two and a half years to binge on city life. Less than that, really, because we *did* have to go to classes and do homework sometimes.

One of my favorite things while I could still see was to go to art museums. I discovered that I had a kind of "hunger" for art. I could never get enough. The museums were, for me, like holy places. My two, going on three, years in the city with my eyesight still working provided me with a storehouse of art—as images in my mind, of course.

Some people nowadays believe that a college education is valuable only if it leads to a good job. The more money you make, the more worthwhile your education was—so the thinking goes. There has always been another way of considering what an education is worth. The old-fashioned way has it that one of the main reasons you go to college is to learn not just *what* to think, but *how*. What is the reason for this? Well, if you learn how to teach yourself, you'll never stop learning, and that's a good and important thing, because there is an endless amount to learn about our world. If you keep learning, you'll be a better, more informed citizen, and you can help make our country and our world a better place for everybody, not just yourself. Also, reading and learning make life richer and more interesting. Books and my many friends who read books and share ideas with me make me happier than just about anything.

My classmates and I loved talking about the things we were learning. Going to college was like opening a chest full of diamonds and rubies and gold, but the real treasure was *ideas*. And we could come up with our own original ideas, our own ways of seeing things around us. This was all so new and thrilling to us that almost every day was an adventure.

But not everything we students learned came from the lips of the professors, or from books, or New York's wonderful offerings. We also learned a lot from each other.

Early in my first year, I met a fellow freshman who was going to become a very important person in my life. He sported a crew cut—a close-cropped haircut that was stylish in those days. He was wearing beige corduroys, an argyle sweater, and white bucks (a suede dress shoe). In other words, he looked like a typical Ivy League college boy from that time. He introduced himself as Arthur Garfunkel. Sometime later, walking back with me after one of our classes, he stopped and asked me to look at, *really* look at, a certain patch of grass.

"Sanford," he said, "let us consider for a moment this patch of grass on the walk. It's of the utmost interest to me, this little grass square. Don't you think it's odd that it comes right up to the concrete, yet doesn't go over it? And why do you think it's green? Grass could be yellow, or even red—and yet it's green. This I find interesting, Sanford."

I didn't know what to say. Arthur was a different kind of guy, that was for sure. I soon learned that he was not being silly or sarcastic when he said those sorts of things. In high school, you could classify a person according to his personality or the group he was in. You could say that a guy was a jock if he was an athlete, or an egghead if he was smart, or an actor, or a goof-off, or an out-of-it guy. I could already tell that guys in college weren't so easy to put in a category.

Then Arthur pointed to the sky and began talking about its color and beauty. I liked this guy right off. I didn't think he was a weirdo, just different from anybody I knew. College was certainly going to be interesting if there were people like Arthur around. I had always been a combination of doer and dreamer. Arthur appealed to the dreamer in me. Little did I know that one day soon he would be part of the world-famous singing duo Simon & Garfunkel. I also didn't know how valuable his friendship would soon be to me.

Arthur and I took a course taught by a professor known to us simply as Goethals. At six feet four, with thick dark-brown hair, Goethals was a hulking presence. Always attired in a good tweed sport coat and a colorful tie tightly knotted to perfection, he spoke in deep, clear tones. His voice was so strong, his speech so articulate, that he seemed to mimic the hero of whom he spoke—the Greek warrior Achilles, or, as Goethals called him, "Akilayoos of the wing-ed feet." When Goethals would recite a passage about Achilles from memory, it was like listening to the author himself—the great blind poet Homer.

Goethals was quoting from *The Iliad*, which tells the story of Achilles and soon became my favorite poem, though I'm not sure whether that was because of the poetry itself or because of Goethals's impressive recitation. I liked hearing it out loud because in ancient times that's how everybody heard it. Even for many years after Homer died, his poems were memorized and recited, until people finally began writing them down. The incredible thing is that *The Iliad* is more than three hundred pages long. Can you imagine memorizing that much? Poets back then must have been like rock stars!

After class, Arthur and I would talk about the things we were reading, about sports, about girls we liked, and about weekend parties. One time before I took a trip home, Arthur, who had never flown in an airplane, talked about what an amazing thing it must be to soar above the clouds. Arthur was like that—like a young child in his ability to enjoy the small things in life. I kind of envied that, but he helped me remember that life is as much about *now* as it is about the future. That was just one of the great things about my friend Arthur.

* * *

So WENT THE DAYS and weeks. One day, as Arthur and I rested on the sundial on College Walk, he hesitantly revealed that he liked to sing. I asked him to sing for me. He was shy about it. To reassure him, I told him that I played the trumpet.

After a short pause, he sang *Bye Bye Love*, a perfect teenage lament about lost girlfriends and loneliness.

"Arthur, that was terrific," I burst out, pleased with his singing and his selection of a song by the Everly Brothers, two of my favorite rock and rollers. "Have you been singing long?" I asked.

"Well, mainly to myself," he said. "When I went to temple with my parents, when I was five or so, I learned some of the melodies. They stuck with me, and after school I sang them to myself on the walk home. I like to walk alone and sing. It's great when no one's around because I can let go. I love the feel of it." This was a guy who would in a few years be singing to audiences of thousands all around the world and selling records in the millions.

"I used to sing the Hebrew melodies to myself, too," I replied. "I was too shy to sing them to others."

He sang a few notes of a different sort of melody, one that I suspect he made up on the spot. It was simple but sweet. Then I joined in and we sang the song together. *Dum dum, dad a dad a dum*—in just those "words." Then, once more. It was a magical moment. Even as I write this, I rerun our singing of that little tune in my mind. Somehow that day combined all the delightful aspects of college life, the pleasures of the city, and, above all, our friendship into one joyful moment, and neither of us ever forgot it.

One late night in our freshman year, Arthur and I found ourselves in a corner booth of a dimly lit restaurant. Tables were scattered haphazardly throughout the room, covered with red-and-white checkerboard cloths. We sat waiting impatiently for some of what was then a relatively new item in American popular cuisine: pizza. This was the first of countless late-night gatherings at the V&T Pizzeria near campus. Our conversations in the past had been mostly tucked in between classes, but now we had the time to sit and talk as long as we liked. Now we could really find out more about each other, our likes and dislikes. He liked thin and delicate women, I liked them more full-bodied; he liked the Phillies baseball team, I liked the Yankees; we both liked a comedian named Lenny Bruce, and we sat there doing imitations of him, cracking ourselves up.

Arthur had a very unusual sense of humor. He was also a natural actor—it wasn't so much what he said as *how* he said it, with funny little accents and facial expressions, that was hilarious. Over time we developed a private, shorthand way of talking and telling jokes; a single word could make us laugh. The word we used for our way of thinking was "crooked." I don't know if we invented that use of "crooked," but it became our own special code word.

There were many such V&T nights, each exhilarating and exhausting, often lasting until well after midnight. But nothing about our friendship up until then was more exciting for me than the conversation we had one day as we strolled casually toward a bookstore on Broadway.

"Now, Sanford," he said, "listen to me. I am going to give you five reasons why you will be my roommate next year." He proceeded to list all five—my nobility, devotion to the arts, and love of beauty were the first three. I was flattered, but, still, there was the problem of our rival fraternities. The next two were the clinchers. "We will form a pact," Arthur said. "Should either of us find himself in need, regardless of the cause, the other will come to his rescue, no matter what." I could tell he meant it, and I could feel it was important; what I didn't know was how crucial that pact would be in the years to come. "Finally," he said, "you're cool."

What? Me? Cool? Though it was uncool then to show too much enthusiasm, I couldn't help a huge smile spreading across my face. We shook on it. As my wise grandmother would have said, it was *bashert*—destined to be.

Arthur and I went to bars in the city; we went to fraternity parties; we went to the pizzeria—and we usually stayed until closing time. We would often still be talking as the sun would begin to come up over the city, vapor rising from manhole covers, buses starting their runs for the day, people beginning to go to work—those unfortunate people who had to. We drank our drinks. We had everything in the world to say, and there was a growing sense that we had very little time to say it.

8

My Roommate

Once we started rooming together, Arthur and I would sit for long hours at our desks working, or pretending to. Arthur would often act up.

"Sanford," he would say, "perhaps you can assist me with my homework. This is a very interesting math problem, don't you think? I find calculus interesting. What would we do without it?" Then he would shout to Jerry Speyer, our other roommate, "Jerry, don't you find calculus really interesting?"

Jerry would come in and shake his head. "What are you talking about, Arthur?"

"Sanford is going to help me with my homework. He's my tutor. Isn't that right, Sanford?"

He would get back to work for a little while. Then he might say, "Sanford, shall I play you a song? Would you like that? I think a little tune is just the thing to pick up our spirits. Reading is good for the soul, but you know, I think music is good for the soul, too."

Then he would play his guitar. People would start coming into our room. Jerry would quit working and come over. Arthur had a terrific voice; everybody knew that, well before he started making tons of money with it. He was serious about his studies, but his music was hard to ignore. I had taken up drums and had managed to bring both my trumpet and the drums to the dorm room. Each night, while Arthur would sing and play the guitar, I would sing and play with him. Full of ourselves, confident of our talents, we made a record together. Rock 'n' roll was *ours*. (Years later, on the occasion of a major birthday of his, I presented Arthur with a copy of that recording. It wasn't half-bad.)

The fall season at Columbia was usually warm and humid. We would open the windows wide so there would be nothing between the room and the sky. Sometimes the sky would darken, and we would know it was about to rain— we could smell it, as if something were coming from the concrete. Then we would hear the rain hit the ground, even from our fourth-floor room. We would go to the window to watch people running for cover, holding newspapers or books over their heads.

In the winter, snow would bring a deep silence, as though the city was made not of iron and concrete and glass but of something soft. We often opened the window for fresh air, and heat would billow from our heating units. And then it would start to *really* snow. Giant clumps would begin piling up on the sidewalks and the window ledges. Arthur would come sit on my desk, maybe not saying anything, just looking out the window, his thin body twisted in order to see.

One day when we were studying the Parthenon, the famous temple of ancient Greece, Arthur said, "Sanford, this is something I would like to see." He tapped the textbook. "I think we should plan a trip and go."

"Well, a trip requires money," I replied. As a scholarship student, I had to work odd jobs to help pay my way. I worked as a waiter at my fraternity, and at home during the summer I was a truck driver, steering a long flatbed filled with bales of old clothing on the two-lane back roads between Buffalo and Jamestown, New York. I had also worked as a door-to-door salesman for the Fuller Brush Company. And I was planning to work as a camp counselor during the coming summer.

"Yes, of course you would need money," Arthur said. "We can save up, and then next year we can go. What do you think?"

I thought it was unlikely, but who was I to spoil his pleasure? "I think it's a great idea," I said.

Then he started musing about how important it was for architects to study the great buildings and how all artists had to create something that would last for a long time. From there he began to wonder what was really permanent in our own lives. Arthur was like that—he could look out the window and see something, anything, and wonder out loud why things were the way they were and how they connected. He was a natural philosopher, and I loved him for it. He wondered if he was cut out to be an architect, and I assured him he could do whatever he put his mind to. He even wondered how long we would be friends, and I told him "a long, long time." (And I was right!)

Then he went over to his desk and took out a black marker. He returned to the window and started to draw on the windowpane. He was sketching the buildings across the street. He drew the skyline in perfect detail, with all the buildings and their windows. Next, he began to draw people: office workers in the buildings, people in the shops, pedestrians on the sidewalks. He drew expressions on their faces, happy ones—he wanted people to be happy. He drew patterns on men's ties and on women's dresses. He made little lines for the sounds coming from the pigeons in the eaves of the buildings, lines to express their motion, too, the way they flapped their wings. He drew plumes of heat rising from people who were rushing about. He drew the clouds. He even drew the stars hiding behind the daylight, and then the shape of the Milky Way galaxy.

"Nice," I said.

"Thanks," he replied.

"How are you going to get that off the window?"

"It's staying forever."

Well, he had to wash it off before the end of the year, but it did stay up for a few months.

Dating

Sue did not, as I had expected, drift away when I went off to college. In fact, we became even closer. She would come to visit me in New York, and we would spend as much time together as possible, enjoying each other's company and going out with my friends. She and Arthur hit it off—he loved her because he loved me and knew she made me happy. It was the same with Jerry. We would go on double or triple dates, taking the girls out for drinks and dinner at the West End Grill, although Arthur and I could barely afford it. Sue would ask me about the girl Artie was with, what she was like, where she went to school.

When Sue was back home, my thoughts and emotions would find expression in letters that ran something like this:

As I suspected, you did go on a date with another guy. An engineering student? Your letter sounded like a goodbye letter, and it is only this that is sad for me. Not the idea of your going out with another man, though I can't say that pleases me. You say you're thinking of me when you're out with somebody else, but is that really true?

I know we agreed to see other people, but sometimes I worry that that is a way of saying it's not going to work between the two of us. Are you sure you really love me?

If I sounded like a lovesick puppy, it's probably because I was. I was responding to a letter Sue wrote to me. Here it is (edited only a little bit):

My Dearest Sweetie:

Well honey, this is the end of a wonderful two weeks; perhaps the most wonderful I have ever spent. I want to thank you for making me so happy during this time and also, most important, for being you. Sandy, I think you know what I am going to say now, and I will continue to say it until I die. I love you. The reason I love you is because you're you. I want you to know that you are all I have ever wanted in anyone. When I think about spending the rest of my life with you, I get a warm glow inside. I think of you as a friend to whom I can always turn, as a kind and loving person, and as a part of me that I never want to lose. I even think about you as the father of our future children.

Sandy, as I said before, and will perhaps say many times before this letter is completed, I love you with all my heart and soul. I am not saying these things because I think they sound good. I am saying them because I mean them more than I have ever meant anything....

10

A Turn in the Road

I had a growing interest in politics, and I was beginning to understand how my family, my hometown, and my state fit into current history. Western New York, along Lake Erie, was then one of the country's biggest industrial regions. Its steel plants and other heavy industries were fed by iron ore brought down the Great Lakes from mines in Minnesota on giant ships, by coal up from western Pennsylvania by rail, and by electrical power from the generators at Niagara Falls. Buffalo, and the nearby town of Lackawanna, was the center of this activity. My hometown had pumped muscle into World War II and was now busy rebuilding the country.

All this purposeful activity gave me a sense of security, which was supported by the quality of our national leadership. Having lost my father when I was five, I had needed a larger sense of leadership and security in my life. If my country was confident, I could be confident.

I knew from my family's table talk how important President Franklin D. Roosevelt had been during the war and how important the overall American effort had been for the Jewish people in Europe. As a boy, I knew about President Harry Truman, who came after Roosevelt; he cared about the working guy—and Buffalo was full of working guys.

Then General Dwight D. Eisenhower became president in 1952, taking the helm of a country poised for even greater prosperity. The century seemed young to us in Buffalo, as if it had been given a fresh start after two world wars. "Ike" Eisenhower stood for stability and strong leadership...until October 4, 1957, when the Soviet Union launched *Sputnik*, the world's first man-made satellite, into orbit around Earth.

It's difficult for an American who was not of age then to comprehend the impact of that event upon the people and the leadership of the United States. We were all stunned. It was almost as if we had been attacked. We—the America of unsurpassed technical know-how and world influence—had been trumped by our new most bitter enemy. In response, President Eisenhower kicked off a grand effort in education and science to restore the country to the top of the technological world. You can imagine a young guy like myself being caught up in the wave of enthusiasm. But you might not be able to imagine the unsettled feeling we all had about the United States and Russia building up nuclear arms as if preparing to destroy the world. I spent more than one sleepless night thinking about all the challenges our nation faced.

Anyway, thanks to my interest in politics, I began traveling around with a college group, meeting with students at other colleges to discuss the important issues of the day. We knew deep down that what we said would probably never reach the ears of our leaders in Washington, DC. But we were preparing ourselves for a life of public service, if we should become so lucky as to be elected to serve our state or our country. Yes, my interest in politics had only grown while I was in college.

I was on my way up—of that I was certain.

* * *

IN COLLEGE, WE READ a lot of stories about the heroes of old and how they sometimes suffered setbacks through no fault of their own. Or sometimes it was their fault. They had some character flaw—their anger or their pride or their jealousy— that would bring them down. The thing is, we took them as great stories about other people. Not about ourselves. Of course, we knew that bad things could happen; we just didn't really see them happening to us. At least I didn't.

But things can come at you out of the blue.

The summer after my sophomore year, I was back home in Buffalo. One evening, as I was pitching in the seventh inning of a baseball game, my vision became cloudy. As I was winding up, the shapes around me—people, trees, blades of grass, the backstop, the red thread on the ball, the hair on the back of my hands—began to vibrate. Vapor seemed to appear in front of me. It was like being in the middle of a very steamy shower. I didn't know what to do. After one of my pitches almost hit the batter, I stumbled to the sidelines and dropped to the ground.

I lay there, my eyes closed in an effort to control the sensation. I felt Sue elevating my head and placing it on her lap. She asked me what was wrong. I said I didn't know. Something with my eyes.

Within a few hours my eyesight returned to normal. The following day, however, my eyes began to itch, so I went to see a local ophthalmologist, an eye doctor. He told me I had allergic conjunctivitis and gave me some drops to apply. But the itching went on, and so a few days later I went to see another ophthalmologist—Dr. Mortson, I will call him— who had been recommended by a friend of the family. He prescribed some different drops. I was to put two drops in each eye daily. I saw Dr. Mortson regularly for the rest of the summer.

In September I returned to Columbia for my junior year. Right away, Arthur noticed that I was having difficulty seeing and reading. But to me it was not a big deal; it was more a nuisance than anything else. I had too much to think about—including all my schoolwork and the upcoming presidential election. One of my professors had suggested that I volunteer to campaign for John Kennedy on various college campuses. So I did. I went all over the place giving speeches.

I used to love to draw. This
is the last portrait I ever
attempted, of my brother Joel.
With my failing vision it took
hours upon hours to finish.

But I had to admit that my vision problems made travel difficult. And that was because my eyesight was, in fact, getting worse.

A few weeks after the start of school, as the Jewish High Holidays began, I attended Yom Kippur services at a synagogue near college. I knew no one there. While I sat in the pew, my vision again came apart, and I began to feel as if I were in a movie, with the cantor and the angels singing the soundtrack. Everything surrounding me seemed to come undone. The lines that separated one thing from another—for instance, the pew in front of me from the altar beyond—blurred and became steamy. I was supposed to be singing and praying, but there was nothing to sing or pray about. I knew then that Dr. Mortson's treatment was either doing nothing or making things worse. I was beginning to get scared.

In spite of my efforts to shake it off, the cloudiness remained. I dared not move. The fog grew worse, and soon I could see almost nothing. I began to panic. By now the other worshippers had left. The synagogue was empty and I sat alone, my head buried in my hands. Finally, a custodian came and escorted me out of the building. His hands were like leather, his voice like breaking rocks.

What was supposed to be a beautiful, peaceful evening had been ruined. I found myself on the sidewalk not knowing which way to go. I knew something terrible was happening to me. I stumbled along, knocking into metal trash cans and a lamppost, the light of which looked like the halo of a launching rocket.

Finally, I staggered over the sidewalk grates next to the college theater. I touched the building, my fingers scraping the coarse concrete wall until I got to the end. I reached out and groped for the iron gates of the university. Victory.

Not until I was in my room did my eyes clear.

I returned to Buffalo in late November to attend my cousin Edith's wedding. As the master of ceremonies, I was expected to read the telegrams that had been sent for the occasion. Waiting behind a drape that curtained off the kitchen from the dining hall, I had to squint painfully in order to memorize the messages so that when I appeared to read them to the group I could do it with no mistakes.

All this time I had been dutifully applying the drops prescribed by Dr. Mortson. Remember, he was a prominent eye doctor—several people had praised his great learning and skill.

My cousin's wedding was also the occasion for a special family event. During World War II, a Catholic family in the Netherlands had hidden Edith's parents from the Germans. Their hiding place for five years was a cramped space under a windmill. As a surprise for Edith, her parents invited to the wedding the father of the Dutch family who hid them.

He turned out to be a tall ninety-year-old man in a black suit and black hat. He spoke no English. Standing before us was a man who, if Edith's parents had been discovered, would've been shot to death, and possibly his family as well.

What was his reward for the risk? Nothing. So why did he do it? I don't really know. I can only say that, when he was introduced, all of us at the wedding felt a swelling in our chests, and not a few tears were shed.

In the presence of this decent and courageous Dutchman, we felt a tenderness that is hard to describe. If you have a loved one whose life has been saved by somebody, at his own risk, you'll know what I mean.

On one crisp and cold night during that visit, snowflakes fell gently upon Sue and me as we started out to dine and dance. We borrowed her father's Ford Falcon. She was well aware by then of the condition of my eyes, but I managed to persuade her that I could still drive. I felt invigorated by the cold air and excited about the prospect of dining alone with her. My doing the driving turned out to be a bad idea.

My night vision was not up to the job. I lost control of the car. Stamping furiously on the brakes, I could hear metal grinding on metal as I hit a parked car, caving in its door. There were no seat belts then to restrain us. Sue and I were thrust forward as our car slid into another car door, bounced off, and went gliding across the snow into yet another car. We spun around in the middle of the street and finally stopped. Sue said she would take the blame, and I let her. I should have done the noble thing, but I didn't need any more trouble. I still had my failing eyesight to deal with, and that was trouble enough.

I never drove again.

11

A Final Exam

After that episode I went to see Dr. Mortson about my continuing vision problems. He told me to keep using the eye drops, and I did, regularly. That was a bad mistake. Normally it's good to follow your doctor's advice. Since this doctor was doing me no good, I should have gone to another doctor. But I was a young man then, too busy to think much about my health.

Back in college, my vision just kept getting worse. One snowy day when I was stumbling about trying to find my dormitory building, I heard some students laughing at me. They probably thought I was drunk. I finally made it to my room and told my roommates about it, and we all thought it was kind of funny. I still wasn't taking my problem very seriously. I guess I thought I would eventually get better. I never

64

thought I would end up completely blind. That was too scary to even consider.

Arthur decided to draw up a chart to measure my "progress." He labeled it "Sanford's Decline in Vision Week by Week" and posted it on the wall of our room. I would stand at a set distance from the sign, and Arthur would ask me whether I could read the letters, which I frequently could not. Each week he saw the problems increase, as did I. And yet I did nothing about it. As long as I could function, I made myself believe, either doctors or my strong constitution would resolve the issue in due course.

As the weeks went by, I had to stand closer and closer to read the letters. Soon, even when I stood very close, I could hardly make out the letters at all. Furthermore, I was getting headaches from my heavy course reading.

Even writing about this now brings back the agony of those weeks and months. Simply put, it was torture. When I was home on breaks, my parents and siblings could see how bad I was, and I hated that. It was embarrassing, but even worse, I could tell that they were worried about me. One of the worst things in the world is having to hide pain so that you won't make your loved ones suffer. I couldn't bear to see them sad on my account.

Arthur and Sue saw the worst of it. But none of us talked much about it. "It" was just that—this thing that was taking over my body. We didn't dare call it "blindness"—we didn't want to give it any name at all. That winter, everyone treated me gingerly, as if I were a thin-shelled egg.

I didn't want to deal with reality. I just wanted everything to go back to normal. I had such a bright future ahead—really, I'd been on top of the world. This vision thing simply could not be happening to me. That was my thinking.

Bit by bit, I could feel things spinning out of control. I stumbled during a dance at my fraternity. I slammed my head on my desk in frustration at not being able to see the blackboard. I nearly fell trying to board a subway car and made a mess eating pizza. It was as if I was spiraling slowly down a drain. I felt alternately tired, headachy, shocked, less than human, ashamed, depressed, and angry. And those are just some of the feelings I had during that bad period of my life.

* * *

NOT SURPRISINGLY, I COULD not sleep the night before the first of the term's final exams, even though I was exhausted from weeks of reading. At nine o'clock on the morning of that first exam, Arthur guided me into a large gymnasium and placed me in a seat in the center of the room. On my desk were a blank blue book and a list of essay questions.

The test began, and once I captured the idea of each question, I wrote furiously. I could not see well enough to make my pen follow the blue lines, so I disregarded them. I continued to scrawl all over the page, for about an hour. Then I glanced at my watch...and saw absolutely nothing.

I shook my head. I blinked. I rolled my eyes. I rubbed them. Nothing helped. I sat still, trying to figure out what to do. Finally, I picked up my blue book and found my way to the front of the room, where I handed it to the proctor. "I can't see well enough to finish," I said.

He took the book from me and laughed. "Son, I have heard a lot of excuses, but this tops them all. I want you to know that you will be graded on what you just handed in."

I repeated that I could not see. As he obviously did not believe me, I started to leave. Watching me stumble back to my chair to get my coat, he seemed to finally comprehend the situation. He took my arm and pointed me toward the dean's office. There, an assistant dean, sitting sternly across the desk, asked me whether I would care to dictate the remainder of my exam. Even though he didn't seem too pleased about it, he was giving me the option of finishing the test orally. I told him that all I wanted to do was go back to my room, pack my bags, and return to Buffalo to see my doctor. He suggested again that I dictate the rest of my exam to him. Otherwise my grade would probably be bad. I was so desperate, all I could do was ask him to please take me to my room. He didn't want to, but he did it anyway.

I called my mother and told her that I had finished my exams early, so I was on my way home. I packed my clothes and, without thinking, gathered up my books. Arthur accompanied me to Grand Central Station, where I could board the train to Buffalo. We said goodbye, and then I felt very alone. I'd told Arthur not to worry about me, but I was worried, and not just because I'd walked out of an important exam. I had a feeling that (1) I would never return to college, and (2) my life would never be the same again. On one of those I was right.

12

Stranger on a Train

I boarded the train and put my suitcase in front of me. It was freezing in the city. Cold air wafted into the car like a ghost, and I pulled my jacket tight around me. A horn blew, and the train pulled out smoothly, as if on air. It would be an eight-hour ride.

It felt as though a door had closed between my present and my future. It was still daytime, but for me it was actually dark, my vision visited by clouds and by what looked like swirling snow. This was deeply troubling: my vision still had not come back to normal, as it had done fairly promptly in the past months.

A man came up and asked if he might take the seat facing me although the car was nearly empty. I wanted to say no, but I said yes. I could tell from his voice that he was perhaps twenty or thirty years older than me. He sat down with a sigh. After a while, he asked why I was crying.

"It's nothing," I said.

"Is there anything I can do?" he asked.

"No, sir."

"I'm a doctor," he told me. "Are you ill?"

"No. Well, sort of."

"I'm an orthopedic surgeon. A bone doctor."

"Oh, it's just a problem with my eyes. An allergy."

"Ah. Well, I did notice they were a little runny."

Embarrassed and a little alarmed, I wiped at my eyes. The doctor told me about a conference he'd been to in the city and how his wife worried when he was away. Then he asked if I had a girlfriend.

"Yes," I said.

"What's her name?"

"Sue."

"That's a nice name. Does she live in Buffalo or New York City?"

"She lives in Buffalo. With her parents."

"Is she in school?"

"Yes."

"That's nice. It must be hard, though, to be away from your sweetie."

I thought of all the letters we had written to each other. "Yes," I said, "it is hard."

"Are you sure you're all right? Your eyes look red, a little swollen." I sensed the doctor moving in closer to examine my face. I felt ugly and ashamed. Without thinking, I pushed my suitcase out with a knee to put more distance between us.

The train was now going through the countryside up along the Hudson River toward Albany. The land, what I could see of it, was mottled with snow and seemed to stretch forever.

The doctor took out a sandwich—peanut butter and jelly—and a small carton of milk and a cookie. I smelled all these things. I began thinking ahead. I would need to get a doctor's note so that I could return to college and finish my exams. I was still sure that my condition was treatable. I would have to tell my mother that I had temporarily lost my vision but that things seemed to be coming back to normal. (At least I hoped so.)

"I would offer you some of my lunch," the doctor said as the train rolled on, "but I'm not sure you would accept it."

"No, no thank you," I said.

"Do you have something to eat? A snack? A candy bar? I think you could buy one if you want. They sell them on the train." I was aware of that, but I did not want to get up and bang myself going through the aisles. My vision was still quite muddy.

"I don't like to see a young man go hungry," the doctor said.

"I'm not hungry, sir. I'm okay, actually. Thank you."

"Still…"

"Really, it's fine."

The doctor broke off half of his cookie. "Here," he said, "take half. I can't bear to see you not eat."

"No, really," I said. I felt as if there was a twig in my throat.

"Honestly," said the doctor. "I have a son. It would upset me terribly if he were hungry and not eating on a train. It's such a long ride. And I can see that you've left in haste."

"I'm fine, sir. I'm okay."

"Please," the doctor said.

I did not answer, but he leaned forward, with half the cookie in his surgeon's hands. I sensed this and was unable to stop myself from leaning forward a bit, too, my long legs pressed up against my suitcase. I opened my mouth, and the doctor placed the cookie partway on my teeth. I took a bite; the sweetness seemed almost unbearable. My stomach was completely empty, and the sugar in the cookie, once I swallowed, hit me with force. I felt as if I had run a long distance and was now at home, relaxed, muscles feeling sore but good.

The doctor took my hand, opened it, placed the rest of the cookie in my palm, then closed my fingers around it. "Please finish it," he said. "If you were my son, I would very much want you to. It would kill me if you didn't. That's what I would want my boy to do."

I obeyed. I was terribly hungry and ate the rest of the cookie quickly. I began to feel strangely happy. My eyes felt as if someone had put a soothing ointment on them.

"I'm glad you took it," the doctor said.

"I am, too."

"Food is a great thing. It's everything, really. I'm a doctor, I should know."

"What's happening to me?" I asked.

"I don't know," he replied, although this was clearly something of a lie. "All I know is that bones grow and then they stop. Sometimes they break. We heal them. They have in them this ability. They have a memory. The body remembers certain things."

"I feel as if I can't remember anything," I said.

The conductor came by and announced that the train was arriving at Schenectady. "This is my stop," the doctor said. "Are you going to be okay?"

"Yes," I said. I truly believed then that I would be. I knew, however, that things would not be easy. My heart felt as if it were wrapped in leather.

The doctor left, but what happened to me next was one of those extraordinary events that take over the mind unexpectedly. The space in front of me, where he had been sitting, was now like a vacuum to me—an absence. I was alone. No roommates, no comforting background noise of fellow students. I was alone in simple fact, yes, but also alone with the gnawing dread about my eyesight, in a panic that suddenly mushroomed. I felt as if I were in an enormous empty, shadowy cavern. Struck with a sudden rush of terror, my mind froze. It seemed there was nothing and no one out there—no world, no past, no future. There was only me, alone and afraid. I felt as if I had turned into stone.

The train began to move. "Going home will be fine," I told myself again and again, as the train made its way closer and closer to...home.

13

Dr. Mortson

When I arrived at the Buffalo station, Sue was there waiting to pick me up. I don't remember what we said. In a few minutes we arrived at my house.

My mother came to the door and gave me a big hug. Before I could remove my coat, my sisters Brenda and Ruth, then six and fourteen years old, attacked me. Brenda jumped into my arms; Ruth gave me a bear hug. Even Joel got in on the action, running down the stairs to welcome me with a big embrace. Brenda had been in the middle of a piano lesson, while Ruth and Joel had happily quit their homework. On previous visits, I would scoop Brenda into my arms, open my suitcase, and place her in it, the others laughing uproariously. Not this time.

The Greenberg Gang — Joel,
Brenda, Ruth, and me.
Without my brother and sisters'
help and love, I never could
have picked myself up off
the floor after blindness struck.

After the hugs, I was able, largely from memory, to place my luggage out of the way by the door and hang up my coat. Entering the kitchen, I quickly sat down, and my mother placed a glass of milk in front of me. When I reached for it, my hand went wide and missed. She tried to pretend she wasn't worried, but the tone of her voice said otherwise. I was too tired to keep pretending. It all poured out. I told her everything that had happened and said that we needed to see Dr. Mortson again as soon as possible.

Dr. Mortson was considered the best in Buffalo, so back to him we went. His voice, like that of many doctors, was very calm and reassuring. All along he had told me to "muddle through" and continue with the eye drops. Now, however, it was finally clear to him that the drops had been slowly poisoning my eyes. He decided to consult with other specialists.

As a result, I was admitted to the hospital in Buffalo, where I stayed until a different kind of doctor was sent to my room. A psychiatrist! Even in my scared and confused state, I knew this was crazy. Dr. Mortson had run out of ideas, or else he was now convinced I was crazy, that my poor eyesight was all in my head. I asked the psychiatrist to please get out of my room, and, with that, I left the hospital.

After further urging, Dr. Mortson consulted with another eye doctor, who then examined me. It was from him that my family and I first heard my condition diagnosed as "glaucoma." We soon learned a great deal about this terrible disease, which is often hardly noticeable at first. It causes abnormally high pressure within the eyeball. That pressure, if not properly diagnosed and treated, may lead to damage of the optic nerve, which sends signals from the eye to the brain and allows you to see.

The dangerous extent of my glaucoma was most likely caused by the very eye drops Dr. Mortson had been prescribing. The drops were a kind of steroid, which can cause a buildup of pressure, and so Dr. Mortson should've been checking that pressure regularly. This was common knowledge at the time. Either Dr. Mortson didn't know, or he forgot. Sometimes the experts can make mistakes, and sometimes the people who are considered "experts" really aren't. I had a rare double dose of bad luck—getting a case of allergic conjunctivitis, and then having Dr. Mortson for a doctor.

My mother and I were soon on our way to see one of the best eye surgeons in the country, Dr. Sol Sugar. He worked at Sinai Hospital in Detroit, Michigan, nearly three hundred miles from Buffalo.

14

At the Hospital

There is a day I will never forget: Monday, February 13, 1961—the day of my appointment with Dr. Sugar.

My mother and I took the train from Buffalo to Detroit, checked into our hotel, and then went directly to Dr. Sugar's office. It was late in the afternoon. The doctor's other patients had left, and we were ushered into his office immediately.

The venetian blinds were open, the sun of a cold winter day streaming in. Dr. Sugar measured my eye pressure using what he explained was an electronic tonograph machine. But the pressure on my eyes was too high for the machine to read! Dr. Sugar was outraged. "Why did they wait so long?" he shouted. "Why did they wait so long?"

My mother and I didn't know how to answer him. By then I was too blind to see my mother's face, but I imagined she was just as confused and upset as I was.

Dr. Sugar then guided me from the examination table to a small, round metal stool. My mother sat in a wooden chair to my right while Dr. Sugar stood above me and put his ophthalmoscope to my eyes. His brow was touching my brow. This man had the hairiest, bushiest eyebrows I'd ever seen (felt). He was looking through each of my eyes to the retina at the very back. Then he pulled away, slowly stood upright, paused for a moment, and said in a flat tone, "Well, son, you are going to be blind tomorrow."

It was as though he were talking to himself. I didn't even know what he meant. How could he know I would be blind? Yes, it was scary, but it was so strange I could hardly believe what he'd said.

I think Dr. Sugar continued to speak, though I don't remember any words after that sentence. He was like a judge giving me a prison sentence. I had assumed he was going to fix my eyes, but here was one of the world's top eye doctors telling me that after today I would never see anything at all. It was too much to take, and so I chose not to believe him. (Deep down, though, I knew he was right.)

Here is what I did. I balled up my fist and stood up to punch Dr. Sugar in the face. Of course, I couldn't see him very well, and my mother was sitting right there, so I sat back down. After all, it wasn't Dr. Sugar's fault—he was just the bearer of bad news. I sat frozen on the stool, clasping my stomach, which was beginning to ache. No one spoke for a long time.

Dr. Sugar began telling us what his plan of action was. "Surgery will be scheduled for tomorrow," he said. And then he was gone.

We hadn't even thought to ask what operation he would be performing. We gathered our belongings and went back to the hotel. When I tried to sit on my bed, I misjudged its position and fell onto the floor, whacking my head. It had been a very bad day.

The next day—Valentine's Day—we went back to the hospital for my operation. Two large men strapped me onto a gurney (a stretcher with wheels) and rolled me into the operating room. Because this was such an unusual case— glaucoma in someone so young—the hospital was going to film my surgery. I also heard someone comment that Dr. Sugar would be writing an article about the case. None of this was reassuring.

Just before I was knocked out with anesthesia, I thought to ask Dr. Sugar what caused glaucoma. He said, "No one knows, and they won't know in my lifetime or yours." He was a man of few words.

"Doctor," I asked, "what operation will you be performing?"

He replied very slowly and loudly, as though I was not only blind but also deaf or mentally handicapped (many people would later talk to me the same way): "Bi-lat-er-al tre-phi-na-tions." I had no idea what he was talking about.

He explained that my glaucoma was so advanced it not only had destroyed my vision, it was on the verge of damaging my brain. I'm glad he didn't tell me exactly what he planned to do. All I knew, as I went under, was that this surgery was absolutely necessary.

I'll tell you about the procedure. If you're squeamish, skip this paragraph. Basically, Dr. Sugar made holes in my eyes. He cut through the delicate mucous membrane covering the inside of my eyelids and then slashed through the wall of each eye to open a channel until fluid began gushing out and forming pools in the wounds. That began to relieve the pressure that had built up. Surgeons back then didn't have the precise instruments they do today. Dr. Sugar used what surgeons today would consider miniature pickaxes. They mutilated my eyes. That was why he knew I would be blind.

The surgery was not a complete success; too much time had passed from the onset of the glaucoma. Scar tissue began to form almost immediately on the walls of the holes in my eyes. That tissue—strong, thick, and fibrous—would eventually clog my eyes' drainage channels. There were more surgeries in my future.

* * *

I HAD JUST BEEN through the two hardest days of my life. I remember looking back and thinking, "God, I did not realize how nice my life has been until now." Yes, I was talking a lot to God during that time, trying not to complain too much, but kind of asking, "Why?"

Losing my eyesight forced me to do a lot of thinking about life and about luck. Most of us don't realize how lucky we are until something terrible happens. I remember a moment one spring day during a high school track-and-field meet. I was taking a break, watching my friends in their events. It was one of those days when the air feels soft. I was lying on the grass, looking up at the sky and then watching my team-mates. I had that good sore-muscle feeling. It was the end of the year. I knew where I was going to go to college. I had a girlfriend. My friends and family were fine. I felt confident and secure. I remember thinking, "It's not going to get any better than this."

Well, in college it did. And then it got a lot worse.

My belief is that the kind of moment I had in Dr. Sugar's office subtracts something from a person. Afterward, you spend the rest of your life building yourself back up, as if something had been cut out of you. And to get back to a feeling of wholeness, you have to work and work at it, as you will see.

Without eyesight, I have developed a very good memory. It not only helps me in my business, it keeps me steady as a person. I can go back to just about any time in my life and find just the right memory I need when I need it. It's like a great big file cabinet in my mind, stuffed full of events and people and places. I go there often to check things. We often rely these days on computers instead of our own memories. We've forgotten that the most complex structure in the universe is the human brain. And it can do amazing things.

Even after that terrible operation, my brain was telling itself, *My life will not be about my blindness.* It was a quiet voice inside me, and I didn't really believe it yet. But it was insistent.

15

After Surgery

When I woke up in my hospital room, I tried to rub my eyes. They were covered with metal pads. I lay there quietly. My mother was sitting in a chair at the foot of the bed. After a while my eyes began to hurt. Then they began to really hurt. It felt as if ice picks were digging into my eyes. I started screaming, and nurses came rushing in. They removed the metal pads, which made it possible for tears to roll down my cheeks. I felt instantly better. The salt in my teardrops had gotten into the cuts in my eyes, causing horrible pain.

The real pain I felt now was not for myself but for my mother. I lay there thinking about what she had just gone through. She had watched her son lose his eyesight. I sensed her suppressing the heaving of her chest. That was probably my lowest moment.

I remembered a time when I was five. Shortly after my father's death, a tall, husky, bearded rabbi wearing a skullcap crouched before me. He took my hand and placed it on the shiny crystal watch encircling his thick wrist. "Look at the hand as it moves past each second," he said. "Once past, each second is gone. It will never return again." He was my Hebrew school teacher back in Buffalo. His words now returned to me.

I wondered if I had been selfish growing up. Had I paid enough attention to my mother and all her hard work to raise and protect her children? Probably not. I had never taken the time to look into her eyes and ask her how her day was. And now I would never see her face again. The seconds had gone, never to return, just as the rabbi had warned. I had missed too many opportunities.

And so, on the day after my operation, what bothered me most of all was not the loss of sight but the loss of *time*. I can't explain it. I just sensed that I had no more time. At least no more time in the light. Maybe you think that I lay there resolving to make every moment from then on count. Well, I didn't. The truth is, I didn't know what I was going to do, and I was too exhausted to do anything but try to get a grip on what had just happened.

Even though the metal pads had been removed, I became conscious of something like a dark-gray metal door on my eyes. From within I could "see" that door, because there was something on it that attracted my notice. There, dancing before me, were a multitude of patterns and shapes. Some of the little figures were gray. Others were black or white. I shook my head in an attempt to clear them. After a while they went away, but they had pointed me toward a new way of perceiving the world. I had begun the process of understanding that I would be able to construct mental images of the faces of the people with whom I spoke. Whether they were accurate pictures didn't matter. I would begin seeing things in detail: the layout of a room and its dimensions and furniture; the color of a person's hair, the shape of his or her eyes, nose, and mouth; images of nature—the sky, the shapes of the clouds, the sunset. And the great thing was that I would be able, in my imagination, to make people and places look as beautiful as I wished.

Despite this discovery, I was not ready to be blind. I was, in fact, very unhappy about it. Who wouldn't be?

They brought me food, but I would not eat. Then they took away my razor blades so I wouldn't harm myself. That first night, I took the sleeping pill I had been given and went to sleep. In a dream I saw that blind beggar in the market from a dozen years earlier. This time he was laughing at me, his head and chest thrown back. Dr. Sugar's words—"Well, son, you are going to be blind tomorrow"—repeated themselves over and over.

Those images and memories were soon replaced by a new one that was also to repeat itself often in my dreams during those early weeks: a large white placard with black letters reading "it can't happen here." Was my mind giving me some hidden message? I think now that it was. I think my mind was telling me, *Okay, if you have to be blind, be blind on your own terms.* In other words, don't be limited by the term "blind person." If that was the case, then maybe there really would be no limits. Well, I knew I would never become an airplane pilot or a sharpshooter, even if I had wanted to. But there was still plenty that I *could* do.

I knew there were things I would have to give up, but I didn't know yet what they would be. I also knew that there would be hard times ahead. But lying in that hospital room, I made a deal with God. "God," I said, "if you get me out of this hole, I'll do everything I can to prevent others from going through grief like this."

At the time I didn't really know what I was committing myself to, or even what "getting out of this hole" meant. I just knew it felt important. It has sustained me ever since, trying to live up to my end of the bargain.

Shortly after this, my rabbi from back home wrote to me. He told me that "a person must never lose hope, no matter how terrifying the future may appear. In fighting tremendous odds, we at least have a chance of making something of ourselves." Those words were a comfort, and I still have his letter.

* * *

I DO NOT RECALL my mother leaving my side once during that entire week in Detroit. Mother was reserved, quiet, thoughtful, and deliberate—a *sabra*, as the Israelis say, like a prickly-pear fruit, tough on the outside, sweet on the inside. The odd thing is that during that time, and even later, my mother and I never talked about my blindness. Besides worrying about me, she was probably also wondering how she was going to take care of me. We didn't even have enough money to pay for the surgery, and now she was going to have a blind young man on her hands. Perhaps she saw my having gone blind as just the next in a long line of hardships, just one more burden to bear.

Maybe if I had been a daughter, we would have talked about my blindness, discussed how we were going to deal with it. But I was the eldest son, and in those days that title came with the responsibility of pretending that things were going to be okay, no matter what happened. So I didn't talk to my mother about my feelings, and, since I didn't, she didn't try to make me.

Back in the early 1960s, when tragedy struck you just had to deal with it. In a way, you still do. No matter how much help you get, you still have to summon strength from within. On the other hand, you *do* need some help. Without the support of my family and friends, I would never have made it. I can't emphasize that enough. If I've learned anything in my life, it's that I'm no good on my own. Maybe some people are—I don't know. I'm glad I've never had to find out.

I can also say that, when it comes to blindness, you need to summon all the creativity you have. The death of my father when I was a young boy gave me a head start in dealing with a setback, but I knew I was going to need more strength and imagination than I ever dreamed I had. Here is one weird thing I imagined before I left the hospital. I imagined that my blindness was like my twin. A big, hulking, sightless person I was going to have to take care of. I was still me, but from now on I would have to go everywhere with this annoying twin. Okay, I didn't want to do that, but maybe over time I could get used to it.

That twin of mine is still with me. I have more or less gotten used to him, or "it." He can still be very annoying (he trips me up on a regular basis, sending me to the hospital for stitches), but I'm no longer afraid of him the way I once was. In fact, he has often come in handy, pushing me to challenge myself, to make me do things I might not have otherwise. At times like this I see that my twin has given me hope. That may sound strange. Without blindness I think I would have had a great life, but who can say? I *have* had a great life, and I have been blind.

16

Homecoming

Another memorable day was the Saturday morning when I walked out of the Detroit hospital. I felt fresh air on my face; I took deep breaths. That moment remains the single most glorious memory of my life.

I was damaged, but not alone. I had been through one of the worst things that can happen to a person. Yet I still had my mind, my body (most of it), and my friends and family. I had reached the lowest point and knew that from now on I was going to work to regain my life. I couldn't know how hard that was going to be. My brain gave me a break by not allowing itself to imagine the struggles ahead.

It was a bitterly cold day when we arrived in Buffalo. Sue was waiting for us at the station. I took her hand and said,

"Your hand is *freezing*." We kissed and hugged, and I could tell she had lost a lot of weight.

The homecoming was awkward. My brother and sisters didn't know what to say to me. That night before I went to sleep, I started to cry. My brother, who shared my bedroom, reached out and touched my shoulder. I was soon asleep.

The following days were filled with visits from relatives, neighbors, and friends. Day after day they came, and day after day we talked about everything—except my new condition. They took their cues from me. I was no longer feeling as hopeful as I had after leaving the hospital. I was tired and had no idea what to do with myself.

Sue would arrive each morning. Her lightheartedness lifted everybody's spirits—except mine. And yet whenever I went to a dark place in my mind, she drew me out of myself. She even persuaded me to attend a friend's engagement party. The idea of exposing myself in what I thought of as my newly deformed state filled me with horror. That was a preview of the rest of my new life. I'm a very social person by nature, but I'm still sometimes embarrassed by my blind "twin."

As it turned out, the party was every bit as unpleasant as I had imagined. Sue stayed by my side, guiding me around the room. Her laughter filled the air, but I could feel, or imagine, that our friends were staring at me. The evening could not end soon enough.

But home and home cooking were sources of great comfort during this time. My mother, Sue, my siblings, and my father did everything they could to make life easier for me.

Mostly I moved around the house and neighborhood by myself...slowly. Heavy black chains seemed to rattle around my body, my every movement limited, cautious, and above all fearful. I wanted to see what I could do by myself, and it wasn't very much. Sometimes Sue would hold my hand and guide me. My only relief came at night when I would drift away into sleep. Try wearing a blindfold all day and you'll have some idea of what the life of a blind person is like. The main difference is that you can take the blindfold off, anytime you want. I can't.

* * *

ONE DAY A SOCIAL worker came to our home to discuss my options for the future. Sue later told me she was a thin middle-aged woman with graying hair. All I could tell was that she was quiet and had no accent.

Sue and I sat side by side like an old married couple. I did feel old—old, tired, and more than a little helpless. The social worker told us we should take a drive out to the country to see some of the blind people she had helped. These people included justices of the peace and men who caned chairs and made screwdrivers. I couldn't picture any of these jobs. How do you cane a chair? Probably something to do with weaving long reeds together; anyway, I wasn't interested in that kind of work or in making screwdrivers. I knew that justices of the peace were not quite lawyers but that they could do some legal work, like perform marriages. So off Sue and I went to meet a justice of the peace.

We drove through little towns and villages. But mostly there were farm fields and forest. It was all very peaceful, but after the excitement of the big city I could hardly imagine sitting out on my porch in a rocking chair, watching the world go by. (By the way, blind people say "watching" the same as sighted people. It just means something a little different. It's all right to ask a blind person if he has "seen" some movie. It would be odd to say, "Have you heard any good movies lately?")

Sue pulled into a gravel driveway in front of a wooden building where we were told there was going to be a wedding. A blind man would be presiding. Sue led me in, and we sat at the back. The justice of the peace was wearing a gray suit and, to hide his eyes, dark glasses. He was marrying a young farm couple, and he didn't sound as if he cared much about it. In fact, he sounded joyless. I was used to big, happy weddings with lots of music and laughter. This ceremony was short and unremarkable. I had a sinking feeling about the whole thing. I thought, "Are you kidding me? I'd rather do anything than this." Well, maybe not rob banks, but still...

I could hear the wedding party walking out of the building and into the dusty air. I could also hear the tapping of the justice's cane against the floor. We went outside and sat with him on a bench. I asked him how he got from one place to another. He said he lived in the village, but if he needed to go farther, there was a bus. I asked, "What if you need to go into Buffalo?" He had no reply. Clearly, he felt the question was strange.

Later, the social worker returned to our house to check on me. Over tea, she asked me how the visit to the justice of the peace had gone. I didn't explain to her that a life like that would actually be a death for me. I listened to her setting her teacup in her saucer. I could hear the floorboards squeak when she shifted. I could even hear her breathe, but I had a weird sense that she wasn't actually there. I admit I was being a little rude, but by pretending to myself that the social worker didn't exist, I could deny that my life had changed. Then I thought, "If I can make her disappear, maybe I can become invisible, too." This idea was strangely comforting, because it helped me mentally set the stage to make the impossible possible. Could I magically reappear and resume my life as if it were normal?

It was only a seed of thought. You *can* make a girlfriend a wife. You *can* imagine traveling. You *can* overlook a setback that snatches away the life you'd been dreaming of. She helped me, that social worker, in ways she probably had no knowledge of. I could feel rebellion stirring in my heart.

17

At the Threshold

Arthur visited me in the spring after my operation. Shortly after his arrival, the two of us were walking down Saranac Avenue. We walked slowly and steadily. For the past several months my body had been tense, almost rigid. I could not even move around my bedroom without knocking into things. Here on the street with Arthur I felt as if there was nothing to knock into. I lightly held his elbow as we walked.

I was uneasy as we began our conversation. I was thinking I might return to Columbia and try to graduate, but I didn't have any idea if it would be possible. In those days there weren't many blind college students, and none at Columbia.

I began telling Arthur about my fantasy of returning to college, and I could sense his blue eyes searching my face.

Arthur interrupted me with a simple question: "When are you coming back?" I told him I didn't know. He said the sooner the better, because I was already several months behind in my work.

My heart soared! He believed I could do it, and he was willing to help me. I began to believe for the first time that the impossible might really be possible. My good friend was telling me that he was willing to room with a blind man, that he would have it no other way. Neither of us knew how much work we were going to have to put in to get me through college—that would all come later. We had made a pact to stick together, and it was being put to the test. If you ever have the luck to be close to someone like Arthur, you will understand the meaning of "a true friend."

We continued strolling along quietly for a while. It had been a few months since the surgery, and my eyes no longer hurt. I could feel the warmth of the sun when we passed between breaks in the trees. I could hear birds and squirrels rustling in the trees, the sounds of life emerging after winter.

I tried to argue with Arthur about how hard this was all going to be. He would have none of it. He began singing, to the tune of the dreidel song: "Oh Sanford, Sanford, Sanford...I made you out of clay, and now you're dry and ready. So, Sanford, we must play." We laughed and put our arms on each other's shoulders.

For a long time afterward I wanted to think it was Arthur who made my return possible, and in a sense that is true. But the door swings both ways. I was going back because of him,

Everyone needs a best friend like Art Garfunkel. When darkness came and pain was all around, Arthur was my bridge over troubled water.

yes, but also *for* him. The meaning of that took me years to fully grasp. In taking, the receiver offers an opportunity for the giver to give. The giver is a receiver, and the receiver a giver. I owe my life to that balance.

We said a lot more on our walk down Saranac Avenue. Though it was quiet out, it was noisy inside my head. I started to think about everything I would have to do to return to Columbia. One thing I knew for certain: my decision would outrage just about everyone. I liked that—not outraging my family, but shocking the people back at school.

But the walk with Arthur was for me the beginning of the end of gray hopelessness. It lifted me out of the grave. I felt as if I had been reborn. I now had a clearly defined goal—a thrilling one. I knew there would be risks, but the possible rewards were great. What I did not know then, of course, were the terrifying and amazing experiences ahead of me. How could I?

Hope is especially meaningful when it is hope for *something*. In my mind I began to struggle toward shaping a course of action. Those thoughts would give me the energy to rise from depression and thus help clear out my feelings of helplessness and self-doubt. It is said that determination to overcome difficulty is a decision. Decisions have to be *made*. This is important.

I could still move. I could go forth. And this time I had a clear direction.

* * *

I HAD YET TO ANNOUNCE my decision to my family. I knew they would not take it well. My mother, especially, would be terrified at sending her blind son off to New York City. In those weeks, she would sit with me at the kitchen table for hours, trying to help me with my coursework, reading complicated material about the law and physics and other subjects she had never studied. It was exhausting for us both, and she probably thought it was pointless since I would not be returning to college. Everyone at home seemed to accept that my days at Columbia were over.

Sue, facing her own college finals, had also been reading to me during those long days and evenings. She knew about my decision, and her support gave me courage. But I needed my family to get behind this as well.

It all came down to one dramatic moment at the dinner table. The scene lives in my memory with exceptional clarity. I quietly informed my family that I had decided to make a full return to the university. There was a long, unnatural silence. I heard Carl's fork fall to his plate. My brother and sisters stirred nervously in their chairs.

"You can't go back," my mother snapped.

Carl started talking in Yiddish as he pushed back his chair, its legs screeching on the floor. "No, no, no. You must stay here. I will not allow it. You will not go back. You're blind, you're blind."

"Carl, stop it," my mother interjected. The more I remained calm, the more upset she became. "Sandy, it would be impossible. Do you understand what it will mean?" She paused. "Why don't you stay here in Buffalo—you could teach, you could get a good job, you could go to work for your father."

I lifted a forkful of mashed potatoes to my mouth and chewed automatically, quivering silently, toes tapping the floor. "I *have* to go back," I said. "Don't you see? I can't stay in Buffalo. There's no future for me here." Then I said something I shouldn't have. "Look at what your God did to me!" I pounded the table with my fist, shattering a plate, and ran toward my bedroom. Carl grabbed my arm, practically dislocating it, and dragged me into the sitting room, my mother on his heels.

He bent my arm behind my back and flung me onto a sofa. Pouncing upon me, he pushed my face into the coarse fabric. My mother was too shocked to speak. "You will not go!" Carl shouted. "You will not go, you will not go!"

My mother pleaded. "Sanford, you can't go back alone. You can't cross the streets of New York. You'll get killed."

Despite my own strength, I could not escape. Then I felt Carl release his grip. Uncomfortable about what he had done, he was nevertheless still angry at me. I had never encountered such intensity from my mother or so much ferocity from my father. Concern for me was the reason—he had always been gentle—but they were also afraid because they knew that I had made up my mind.

* * *

ON A WARM DAY in the early fall of 1961, my mother and I took a taxi from the airport to Columbia University. As we approached the campus, my mother described the crowded streets and the old buildings that I knew so well. The day I had hoped and fought for had arrived, and I was scared. I slouched down, my heart sinking. I wondered if I was making a huge mistake.

My mother came with me only as far as my old dormitory hallway. There was no one else about, just the pale concrete blocks—and me. Mother and I said a quick goodbye. A kiss on the cheek, and she was gone. I didn't want to picture what was in her heart just then. I had my own immediate problems.

I felt my way down the hall. Then I was standing at an old wooden doorframe that I could feel was gouged and dented from the comings and goings of generations of students. A threshold. There was nothing behind the door except my old room. All I had to do was open the door and walk through.

I could still turn around, I thought, make it down the hall and outside to the street with my old green suitcase, hail a cab, pick up my mother at her hotel, and return to the airport. We'd be in Buffalo by nightfall.

If I went into my dorm room, there was only the *possibility* of a life. Also the possibility of a great failure—a life filled with danger, humiliation, falls, injury, maybe even death. If I opened that door, I would have to go into the room. If I walked into the room, I would have to put my suitcase down. I would stand there alone. The room would smell musty, from the dust burning off the old heaters. I would have to unpack, feel my way around to the dresser, open the drawers, and put away my clothing. I would painstakingly struggle to separate my underwear from the socks, the T-shirts from the slacks.

I thought about my old Buffalo neighborhood and how I knew it by heart. I knew the neighbors' faces and the positions of the trees, the lawns, the stores, and the junkyard. Everything was in its proper place. What did I know of New York City after two years? Proportionally very little. The city was of gargantuan scale and ever changing. If I stayed, I would have to conjure an image of everything I would ever confront: every building, everything I touched, every book I read (correction: that was read *to me*), every face, every hand I shook. I would have to marry voices with my own images of people I had never seen. Was my imagination capable of this? Would my mind be able to retain and process it all? And Sue would probably *not* wait for me, I thought. She might get an opportunity to pursue her education elsewhere, far from Buffalo. What woman would want to wait for me to take her elbow so that *she* could open doors for *me*, lead me around rooms, make sure I did not eat the garnish, make sure my clothing matched? The list of difficulties rolled on and on in my thoughts. My stomach hurt.

If I stayed, my downfall would just be a matter of time. I would be doomed. To live a new life outside the safety of home was the only path forward for me, but could it be done?

There was still no one else in the hallway. The other students were not back from vacation, and the campus had a hollow feel. Soon they would all return, eager to get back into the swing of things: going to classes, football games, and fraternity parties; exploring the city and getting into trouble.

That part of my life was over, and I knew it. There would be no free time. I would have to work on my studies during all my waking hours—and almost all of my hours would be waking ones. If there was any time left over, say, at two or three in the morning, I would use that time to write to my family and Sue.

Standing alone in that hallway, I realized that I had never before this moment known real fear. There was a harsh taste in my mouth. My hands and legs were actually shaking. I was thinking, "I...can...not...do...this." My fingers ached in anticipation of all the hurt they would encounter. I could hardly breathe.

I opened the door.

I stood for a while in the open doorway. I was deluged by memories of those sleepless nights during the past school year, with pain in my eyes so sharp I thought they would burst from their sockets. The cold packs on my eyes, the pacing of bare feet on the cold floor. And now here I was, in the same room, a different person.

I walked in, my heart pumping with fear and excitement, and set my suitcase down. The room did smell musty. I touched each thing in the room, slowly and carefully. Everything seemed to be exactly as it had been when I had left in a panic. How could that be? I sank into the large, soft leather chair, which was just where it had been before. I felt the burden of the world on my shoulders.

18

The Blind Student

My first days of classes as a college senior were nerve-racking. I was so intent on concentrating during the lectures that I froze. In trying to remember every single word the professor said, I remembered almost nothing. I walked away from classes each day with my mind tied in confusing knots of sound.

Gradually, though, I began relaxing, and with the help of a tape recorder, I started getting the hang of it. I began to open up my brain the way a fish opens its gills—it does this or it dies. I memorized virtually every sentence read to me that year, something I did not know I was capable of. Instead of cramming before an exam and then dumping the information and forgetting about it, I had to absorb material in a way I never had before. I still remember much of what I learned then. Acquiring knowledge at such an insane pace has been a continuous wonder and joy for my life within my mind.

In order not to waste a single moment preparing for classes, I saddled myself with anything and everything I thought might be useful. I purchased all the required books and then some, as well as dozens of blank recording tapes. I looked for readers among my friends and acquaintances. I called up all the institutions for the blind to request volunteer readers. (I will forever be deeply grateful to those readers, at Columbia and in my later studies. They made possible the life I was trying to build back for myself. Many became dear friends for life.)

With all these people I was able to set up a very complicated schedule of meetings. Except for classes, my day was filled with readers from 8:00 a.m. until midnight. I set aside no time for breakfast but reserved ten minutes for lunch and a half hour for dinner. Weekdays from midnight until 2:00 a.m., as well as Saturday nights, were reserved for listening to tapes. I wanted to feel secure, so I clutched at everything.

My elaborate scheduling did not work quite as planned. Many of my readers did not show up as promised. Others came late. Some came at the right time but on the wrong day. Still others came on the right day but at the wrong time. There could be four-hour stretches with no readers, and then several would show up for the same one-hour period. They were human, after all, but it was discouraging for me.

Things did improve by the second week, but there were still problems. I needed assistance getting around campus, and people weren't always there when I needed them. In spite of his own demanding schedule, Arthur remained my strongest and most reliable source of support. True to our pact, he always came to my rescue. Sue helped as well, regularly sending me readings on tape.

I had some study notes I made in very large, thick black letters, which I could read with the shred of sight I still had. But soon that shred was gone. From then on it was me and my trusty tape recorder. There were no microcassette or digital tape recorders back then, so my parents bought me an expensive reel-to-reel machine. It was big and heavy, and I hated it. I felt chained to it, but I had no choice. It was almost as big as a small roll-on suitcase you might store in an airplane's overhead rack, but without the wheels, and when its top was opened, another two feet by one-and-a-half feet was added to any surface. I had to haul that thing all over campus. But it gave me a little bit of independence—I didn't have to rely completely on readers.

I heard those taped voices in my sleep—when I did sleep. In my dreams there was now the hum and winding of the tape recorder; the tape rolling over the reels, sometimes getting caught; and the snap of the off switch.

I set outrageously ambitious deadlines for myself. And still I worried. Determination does not always prevent self-doubt.

One Saturday that fall I went to a football game with a bunch of my friends. Everything was fine for the first quarter. We were all having a grand time. Then somebody had to go get a hot dog or use the restroom, so we all had to stand up. At that point a person behind us accidentally knocked into me, and I got pushed forward a little bit. I reached out to steady myself on the back of the person sitting in front of me. But he was gone. I toppled over the bleachers for a row or two. I didn't break any bones, but I did need stitches.

It was a trivial incident, but I felt like a fool. On the other hand, it helped steel my determination. It was just one of many, many times I would need stitches.

* * *

AFTER I GOT SOMEWHAT used to my crazy schedule, I began to think about what I would do after college. The prospects did not look promising. I assumed that the better graduate schools, especially the law schools, would not accept a blind student. I had always wanted to go to Harvard Law School, so I traveled up there to talk with the dean. Arthur went with me. He told me that the dean was a giant with a wide mouth and fat cheeks and that he never smiled. I asked him what advice he might have for me. He told me that I should continue with my studies but not think about law school for now. Well, at least it was not an outright "no."

Back at Columbia, I began to apply instead to PhD programs in government studies and international affairs. I decided to hedge my bets and apply to as many graduate schools as I could, seven in all. Arthur helped me with the application process, as did Sue. We decided to inform the

schools straight out that I was blind. Then we worked fever-
ishly to meet the deadlines.

Meanwhile, the daily challenges of my condition continued
to turn everyday activities into sometimes daunting adventures. After meeting with one of my professors about my
future, I was heading back across campus by myself. I was not
using a cane because I didn't want to show the world that I
was blind. When I started down the concrete steps next to
the statue of Alma Mater, I stepped too far and went crashing
down. My head was bruised, my pants torn, and my sport coat
and shirt covered in blood. I got up, happy that no one seemed
to have seen me, and hobbled back to my room.

* * *

HERE IS WHAT ARTHUR did for me after I returned to college:
He fixed the tape recorder when it was broken. He read to
me every day, often for several hours. He filled out my graduate school applications, and he kept audiotapes of them (so
I could refer to them if necessary). He spread out my papers
on the floor, and he and I would map out my work like spies.
He walked me to and from classes. He escorted me across
the city. He bandaged my shins when I bloodied them, which
was often. He also bandaged my forehead and my knuckles,
getting my blood on his hands and under his fingernails. We
were like brothers. He did not say anything about his help,
though I knew he did not like the sight of blood.

When he walked me to classes, we walked as if nothing
was wrong, and we talked along the way. People who didn't

know my situation must have thought it odd to see a college student holding on to another. But Arthur didn't mind.

Arthur was a devoted student of architecture, which took a lot of time and attention. He was also an artist, a poet, a singer, and a guitar player. Sometimes when I studied, I could hear the slow drag of his pencil against paper. He would often sing to himself while he worked. I don't know what made him change his mind and decide to switch from architecture to pursue a much riskier line of work—singing. It turned out to be a great decision for him, but it took a leap of faith, just as it had taken a leap of faith for me to return to college.

I will never know exactly what Arthur gave up to help me and what he got from it in return, other than my undying devotion. One of the things he gave me as a friend and roommate was his simple presence. The sound of his breathing at night was reassuring. As a blind person, you have to pretend that everything is okay when it is not. Having a person nearby who cares about you is crucial. Arthur understood this very well.

Last but not least, there were his words of encouragement, the expressions of faith, the expressions of knowing something that was impossible for him to know but sounding as if he did.

I am indebted to Arthur in a way I can never repay. That is hard to live with. Yet I have learned to accept my good fortune. You see, I was beginning to realize that the terrible misfortune of going blind was slowly turning into something bigger and more beautiful than I could have realized. My good fortune was to develop the kind of deep friendships that I think are rare in life. And deep friendships are one of life's greatest treasures.

19

Miss Borlak

At the end of October, I had an appointment at what I will call the Institute for Blind Persons. I wanted to see what they might recommend to help me in my daily life. The place was in the middle of the city, so Arthur went with me.

I was introduced to a Miss Borlak (not her real name), who was to work on my "case." She had a high-pitched voice and wore perfume that smelled like dry grass. Arthur told me later she wore glasses and purple lipstick.

She asked me some questions about my life and routine. Then out of the blue, she said, "How do you like being blind?" I was taken aback. It seemed a little blunt, if not heartless. However, since I was asking her for help, I felt I should answer.

"To be frank, I don't like it," I said. "The fact is, I dislike it very, very much." I told her about the problems I was having in adjusting to my new life.

"Let me be a little more specific," she continued. "Do you consider yourself to be a blind boy?"

That seemed an odd question, but I answered, "Well, in the sense that I can't read or move around by myself, I guess you might say that I'm blind. I don't think it's all that important whether or not I consider myself blind."

"It *is* important," she replied, "particularly because it affects your attitude toward life, and now you have a whole new life ahead of you." She was toying with me, in a way. I was being defiant. Although she understood my attitude, she was angry that I did not appreciate her help.

When the half-hour session was over, I left in an uneasy state of mind. For some reason, in the heat of the moment, I had blurted out that I didn't think it was important for me to consider myself blind. My struggles in the last few months had given me the strength to say that. Could I now live up to it?

At our subsequent meetings, Miss Borlak wasted no time with small talk. She got right to the point: "Now, tell me, do you consider yourself to be blind?" Her aggressive tone only made me more defiant. I thought these sessions were supposed to deal with practical problems of daily living, not with my state of mind. I did not know how to respond.

"Because I can't easily travel about by myself, I often travel with someone," I replied. "I don't think this is an unusual way to handle the problem. I haven't begun to perfect all the techniques that I'm sure would be useful, and that's one of the reasons I'm here."

I sensed her impatience. "That's precisely my point," she said. "You won't admit you're blind. You do everything you can to avoid being a blind person. You *are* fortunate in that your blindness is not as obvious as it is with most others. You are able to focus your eyes on objects, or at least appear to be able to. But the plain fact is that you are blind."

I winced. The words came across as harsh. She continued, "You're trying to do everything you used to do, as though nothing happened. If there are inconveniences, you drag people in to help you. Every week you come here with your friend, and you think nothing of it. Is he or someone like him going to travel around with you for the rest of your life? You take about two hours out of his life each time you come here, and I can't even begin to think of the many other hours you demand of him."

Now I was annoyed, and she knew it. She thought she was prodding me in the "right" direction. "Miss Borlak," I said, as politely as I could, "my relationship with Arthur is a personal matter." I paused, then said, "I can see the point you're trying to make."

"Don't you think," she went on, "it would be easier for those around you if you could travel independently? Wouldn't that restore your pride?" I was unhappy about that suggestion, but I thought about it anyway. "As you probably know," she said, "blind people have other means of traveling. One of the most popular is a dog. They are wonderful companions, perhaps even more loyal than humans. The institute could make arrangements to procure one for you. A dog can become a best friend."

"I already have a best friend," I said. I thought about relying on a dog and how degrading that would be. A dog would proclaim my blindness. Moreover, I would come to depend on the dog. No, I would not use one—I would remain independent. President Franklin D. Roosevelt—crippled from polio—had always been a model of how one handles a disability. You carry on as if it doesn't exist.

"Or, if you would prefer," Miss Borlak said, "you could try a cane. Unlike dogs, canes don't require upkeep. We could get you the most modern, lightweight collapsible model." I was still reeling from her comments about a dog, so the idea of a cane suddenly made me deeply sad. I asked her if we might discuss this again next week.

Arthur and I left and stepped into the warmth of the sun. He must have seen my pained expression and remained silent. Miss Borlak had touched upon one of the painful truths of my situation. It was indeed inappropriate, even unfair, to burden my friends, and in particular Arthur. I could not easily travel alone. In many situations I did require assistance, which was at times seriously inconvenient for my friends. Since I could not bear the thought of a dog or a cane, I remained torn about asking friends for help. Somehow I had to deal with this problem or it would extend throughout the rest of my life.

At what turned out to be my last meeting with Miss Borlak, in the spring of 1962, I went into her office the same as I always had. Arthur brought me in and sat me down gently. I had an obvious scrape on my head from having bumped into something. She asked me whether I had changed my mind and had accepted the fact that I was blind and was going to have to change my life.

"I don't want a dog or a cane," I said.

"You don't even want to admit that you're blind, do you?"

"Well, I'm not," I said.

"What do you mean you're not? Of course you are." Her voice rose. "You're blind. And you need help. This is the Institute for Blind Persons. You came here for our help. You just don't want to look at reality, that's all. Listen, if you want things to work out, you have to accept reality. You need to understand that."

I didn't say anything for a time. I just sat quietly. Suddenly, something soft and heavy brushed against me. It was a dog. The door had opened and a man, a dog at his side, had entered the room. I began to perspire. The dog was breathing heavily. Miss Borlak said, "I thought you would like to see how a blind man travels independently." I tried to remain calm, but I began to panic. I didn't dislike dogs, but we never had one growing up, and I didn't like the idea of one being thrust at me.

I slid my chair back toward the wall, and the blind man moved toward me. He groped for my hand and placed it on the dog. "You're blind, young man!" he shouted. "You must use a seeing-eye dog. This is your first lesson. Get up!" I jerked backward, striking my head against the wall. "Miss Borlak, I have to go. Where's Arthur?"

Arthur and I rushed out of the building. I told him that the meetings were becoming intolerable. "What's going on?" he asked.

"They want me to use a dog! They might as well give me a tin cup and sunglasses and sit me on a street corner." I clung lightly to Arthur's elbow as we made our way out to the sidewalk.

20

The Subway

One of the most important episodes in my life happened after I left Miss Borlak's office that final time.

Arthur suddenly remembered that he had to do a sketch of a famous building downtown, and so he couldn't go back up to the campus with me right away. I was expecting a reader there in an hour, so I had to get going. Neither of us would budge. Finally, I said, "Okay, then, I'm going by myself."

"Are you sure?" he asked.

"Yes," I said. I felt that I was being abandoned, but I shrugged it off and began to make my way down the sidewalk as though I was part of the crowd.

Arthur was gone. I would have to take the subway back up to the campus by myself. I could have hailed a taxi, but as a scholarship student I hated spending money unnecessarily. As you've probably figured out by now, I was also stubborn.

I began to walk in the direction of what I thought was the subway entrance. I put my arms out and moved like a zombie. People must have given me strange looks. I felt people's elbows and backs. Then a young woman asked me where I was going. I told her. She asked what was wrong. "Nothing," I said.

"Clearly, something is wrong."

"No. I'm just having a little difficulty seeing. If you could point me in the direction of the subway, that would be a big help."

She walked along with me, touching me here and there to make sure I did not step into the street. Then she gave me the directions, explaining how many steps this way and that way. She was worried about me, but I assured her I was okay. I didn't want her to leave, but I couldn't tell her that.

I felt my way along the edge of a building until it disappeared and the street became quieter. My foot went into the breast of a pigeon; it chuckled and moved out of the way. I felt sorry for it. My hands were now gritty from pressing them against buildings.

I came to an intersection I needed to cross. There weren't any audio signals for blind people back then. I ended up walking straight into a man's chest. I bounced off him and fell to my knees. "I'm sorry," I said.

He reached down with one hand and lifted me off the pavement with astonishing ease. "No, it was me," he said. "It happens all the time."

"What happens?"

"I take up too much space," he said. "It's hard for me to get around. Not that I can't move—I can, but other people seem to fall into me." I pictured a giant. "I'm a fighter," he said.

"You mean a boxer?"

"Yeah."

"That must be hard."

"It's hard to get beaten on every day. But winning is fun." He had a light voice. "You seem to be having some difficulty," he said.

"Maybe a little. It's just that I can't see. Can you tell me where I am?"

"New York," the man said.

"Am I close to Grand Central Station?"

"Very close. Right across the way there."

"Can you point me in the right direction?"

Then the man did something amazing. He took me by the shoulders and turned me right in the direction of the station. It was such a gentle movement that it was hard to believe he was a fighter. I could hear the noise of a crowd coming from over there. "Thank you," I said.

I left him and walked across the street and into the station. I found a railing and hung on to it as I made my way down into the cavernous main area of the terminal. I would have to find my way to the crosstown shuttle train to Times Square. Then I would have to change to the uptown Broadway train, which would take me some seventy blocks north to

Columbia. It gave me a sinking feeling. I asked someone how to get through the central hall to the shuttle area.

Being told directions is one thing; following them, when you are blind, is another. I knocked into benches, brief-cases, and people. I kicked over coffee cups. The skin on my shins got split open; I felt blood wetting my socks. My knees seemed to be swelling, probably because I was banging them into everything. All I wanted was to get out of that pit.

Fortunately, I recalled some landmarks from my days with vision, and fellow travelers helped me. By bumping into people and asking questions, I made it to the general boarding area, put my token in the slot, and pushed through the turnstile. That felt like a huge accomplishment.

As I was walking toward the track, I bumped head-on into an iron column. My outstretched arms missed it completely, but my face did not. Blood poured down my forehead. I swiped at it with my forearm. It hurt, but the greater pain was embarrassment. I wished that because I could not see people, they could not see me.

I swung around toward the subway track. It smelled greasy and oily. I began shuffling, little by little, toward the platform. One foot was just over the edge, and then came a terrifying sound—a train roaring through the tunnel. I lunged backward, and slammed into the column again. It was like being hit by a big frying pan. The ringing in my head seemed to course through my body. I put my arms out again and pushed into a woman's breast.

"Pardon me!" the woman said.

"God, I'm sorry," I said. "I didn't see you."

"That's a first," she replied. "But you look like a nice boy. There's a cut on your head." She put her hand to my forehead.

"It's nothing."

"Well, good luck. It's always hardest at first," she said, "but then it gets easier, I think."

She continued on her way, leaving me wondering how she knew. Was she talking about blindness? About new things in general? Or just life itself?

Feeling a little better, I started moving more quickly, slammed into a baby carriage, and fell onto the concrete. I think the mother caught the baby. She said something I could not understand. It sounded angry. I couldn't blame her.

When I got to my feet, I apologized. It was becoming clear to me that I would never make it back up to Columbia. I walked until I stumbled forward. My hand reached over a ledge, beyond which was the space where the train would arrive. I thought, "I could be killed by a train."

Then, I suddenly realized that my friends and family were counting on me. The idea came on me in a flash—*they* were counting on *me*. Because they cared about me, they needed me to take care of myself. I had a responsibility to them. That glimmer of insight helped me begin to see how pointless it was to try to hide my blindness from those closest to me. I wasn't protecting them; I was just protecting my foolish pride.

The train was coming. I got up, boarded with the others, and heaved a sigh of relief. When my knees pressed against a seat, I sat. I was halfway home. My legs were still bleeding but my head wasn't. The train echoed under the city.

By this point I knew I would never make it back in time for my appointment. My goal now was simply to get back to my dorm in one piece. Then I smelled a familiar odor—something pleasant. I didn't know what it was. Anticipating the next stop, I got to my feet and stumbled onward, dodging people and posts.

When the train ground to a halt at Times Square, I didn't want to get my foot caught in the gap between the train and the platform, so I took a giant step out. I jostled into another man, and there was again the sense of something familiar. It was like a ghost. I moved along with the crowd to find the platform for the train heading to Columbia. When a train came, I got on, hoping it was the right one.

I was completely exhausted. I felt half-crazy. Why had I done this instead of just staying downtown with Arthur? Then I thought about my grandmother and my parents. Nothing—poverty, fear, disease, or war—had deterred them from their emigration across Europe and the Atlantic Ocean. As hard as my little underground excursion was, it was trivial compared with theirs.

Still, in its way, it *was* hard. My stop was finally announced, and my weary feet took me to the top of the steps and out on the street. From there, I felt my way to the iron gates and went through onto College Walk. I don't think I was ever happier to find myself back at the university. As I began to make my way, I was stopped by a young man I recognized by smell as Arthur.

"Excuse me, sir," he said. Then, "*I* knew you could do it... but I wanted to be sure *you* knew you could do it." He had been shadowing me all along! He later admitted that he had not needed to do that sketch after all.

We were silent for a moment. I think my first words were, "I'm going to kill you." Then I grabbed his hands, raised them, and swung him around me. We went waltzing along in big, crazy, happy spirals. I felt drunk and giddy, and so happy to be alive.

I had survived! I had triumphed over an ordeal, and over fear as well. Fear of risk and movement and change—all of these were defeated in that subway journey. And here's the really important thing: They were defeated not by me alone. I saw that my friends and family had become angels who would be with me and never leave. I was strong because of the strength we gave each other.

Graduation

S pring of senior year was coming up fast. I was not looking forward to it. Every day Arthur would go to the mailbox looking for letters from the graduate schools I had applied to and come back empty-handed. I began getting a daily stomachache. I was fairly certain I was not going to be accepted by any of the schools—yes, I had very good grades, what with all my grinding work, but, well...I was blind.

Still, I had hope.

The first letter I received was a rejection. Holding the letter like a dead mouse, I took it to the professor who had written me a recommendation. I sat in her office while she called the school that had rejected me. The dean there answered. My professor started yelling, "What gives you the right to reject Greenberg? He's met all of your requirements and then some."

A dreadful pause. The man probably responded he didn't think I could handle their reading loads. After a few more choice words, my professor slammed the phone down. She consoled me, and I staggered back to my dorm.

I had been invited, along with some other seniors, to a party where we would have a chance to meet former president Dwight Eisenhower. His extraordinary accomplishments both as general in command of the Allied invasion of Europe in World War II and as US president made him an early hero of mine. He had also served as Columbia's president. Almost as soon I entered the room, a military aide took my arm and escorted me to a back corner. There stood the man who had charted perhaps the greatest military victory of the century. I was introduced, and I could tell he was extending his hand.

"Mr. President," I said, "it is an honor to meet you."

"Thank you, Sandy," he replied. Since I couldn't think what else to say, he continued. "I understand that you have excelled at this university of which I am so proud." He went on to tell me that, like me, much of his life was spent fighting the odds. He had served for sixteen years as a major, he said, before he was promoted to lieutenant general. Sixteen years! That was nearly as many years as I was old.

"There were many who underestimated me," he said. "Many of my setbacks were not short-lived, either. Despite them, I never lost confidence in myself." His presence and his story moved and inspired me.

But by the time I got back to my room, I remembered that I'd just been rejected by a top graduate school.

* * *

ONE DAY ARTHUR CAME back from the mailbox with more letters from graduate schools. "The results are in," he said. "Would you like me to read them to you?" Although I could hardly bear the thought of being humiliated in front of my friend, I had no choice.

"Is there one from Harvard?" I stammered. "Open it, please." The sound of him undoing the envelope seemed to go on forever. Arthur stood up and in an exaggerated British accent read, "It is with great pleasure..."

Harvard wanted me to join their graduate program in government. The letters from the other schools were more or less the same—I'd been accepted at all of them—but we both knew I'd be going to Harvard. I fell back on my bed, overwhelmed, as Arthur laughed.

I couldn't believe my good fortune. One moment I had been scuttling along with my studies. Now, somebody was telling me that all that work was worth it—I could go on, keep dreaming big.

There was more good news. I was elected president of my class. Before I knew it, graduation day had arrived. As class president, I had to stand in front of all my classmates and professors and their guests and give a speech. The podium was positioned in front of the statue of Alexander Hamilton. I stood as straight as I could. It was a soft spring day, the smell of recently cut grass heavy in the air. Behind me sat the dean of the college.

The audience quieted, but I remained silent for a moment. This spot, sheltered from the surrounding city, had been the heart of my college life. I could not avoid thinking of how much my life and I had changed since my high school graduation four years earlier.

The wooden chairs creaked and clattered. The click of a nearby camera caught my notice; I supposed that Sue's father was taking a picture. I began to speak...

22

A Wedding and Graduate School

There's so much more I would like to tell you. Sue and I got married that summer after we had both graduated from college, for instance. I'd like to describe how beautifully Arthur sang at our wedding and how, as the band played the *hora* (a circle dance often done at Jewish weddings), the guests lifted this new husband and wife up on chairs and bounced us until we were dizzy.

I'd like to tell you about how hard and exciting graduate school was at Harvard—how Sue went to work teaching special-needs children while I dug into my studies again. At Harvard I managed to create a recording device that compresses speech by eliminating random milliseconds

Sue and I dancing at our
wedding, just as we did at
our prom four years earlier,
but with one big difference:
Now I am blind.

of sound in sentences so that anyone who needs to absorb large amounts of recorded speech can listen to two to three hundred words or more in a minute without distortion. An ordinary tape playback could only reproduce one hundred words per minute. I later sold the rights to that technology and made enough money for us to live on. (A digital version of the same technology is used today for everything from MP3 music downloads to Audible on Amazon.)

During our time at Harvard, I received a scholarship to study for a year at Oxford University in England. It was too great an opportunity to pass up, but the main thing I remember about Oxford is how cold it was. The library was big and cold; our apartment was small and cold; everywhere we went, it seemed, was gray and cold as stone. Growing up in Buffalo, I thought I knew about cold!

One day while we were in England, I got a call from Arthur, who was now in architecture school. "Sandy, I'm really unhappy," he said. "I don't like doing this."

"So what is it you want to do?" I asked.

"You remember my friend Paul Simon? We want to try our hand in the music business, but we need four hundred dollars to get started." Arthur never got around to exactly what he and Paul needed the money for—a demo tape maybe, maybe a guitar, who knows—but I didn't care. I sent the money off to Arthur immediately, even though doing so just about emptied our savings account. The debts that really matter often can't be measured in dollars. This was one of them.

I invented this weird looking
contraption to compress speech
and play it back at high speeds
for my own use, because blind
people can process sound much
faster than those with sight.
Eventually, I sold the rights
to the technology for quite
a lot of money

That four hundred dollars and the careers it helped launch turned out to be an important footnote in the history of contemporary music. Instead of Tom & Jerry, the band name Paul and Arthur had used in high school, they used their last names this time. According to *Rolling Stone* magazine, Simon & Garfunkel is one of the top forty recording artists of all time, right between the Doors and David Bowie if you know your rock 'n' roll history. But I didn't give Arthur the money because I expected that or even cared. He had restarted my life, so I would help him restart his. I was happy to do it.

As I keep saying, that's what true friends are all about.

I would also like to tell about how I ended up a White House Fellow, working under President Lyndon Johnson for a magical year; how I started a number of companies that were very successful and have helped Sue and me live a very comfortable life. I could you tell you about my three children, of whom I'm very proud, and my four grandchildren, of whom I'm even more proud. (Grandfathers can get a little sappy!)

I could tell you about the famous people I've known, about how I've collected art all my adult life even though I can't see it—works done by famous artists like Rembrandt and Picasso and Frank Stella—and even about how I still play basketball sometimes. I can sense from the waves of people around me where the net is, and I guard and shoot accordingly. I even make a shot sometimes. But I suspect what you would really like to know by now is what it's like to live without sight, to get along in the world as a blind person. So I'll go there next.

I've never seen my sons
Jimmy (left) and Paul, or
my daughter Kathryn,
but in my mind's eye I
know exactly what all
three look like.

Is daughter Kathryn leading
me? Or am I leading her —
and if so where? This photo
always reminds me of
three-year-old John F.
Kennedy Jr. saluting the
casket of his slain father.

23

My Daily Life

I wake up before my wife and take a shower, gripping the bar of soap tightly. If it slips out of my hand, I have to bend down and search for it. I am tall, so this is not easy. Sometimes I cut myself shaving, but I don't always know it. I rely on my wife to tell me.

Then I stand in my dressing room knowing that my suits are on one side, my wife's things on the other. On my dresser lies everything I will need for the day—cash, wallet, keys, cell phone. My things are arranged in neat piles—for example, a stack of one-dollar bills, a stack of fives, and so on. I put each stack in a different pocket of my specially tailored suit, and then I use the bills for tipping doormen. My wallet is thin and neat, and I know, by touch, where each of my credit cards is. Like a magician, I am able to pull everyday personal articles out of hidden places.

I like to look as sharp as a newly minted coin, but if you were to see me in bright light, you would notice that on my forehead there are tiny lines—scars from all the times I have run into walls, columns, and corners. There are also scars on my elbows, shins, knees, and feet. These things are part of the cost of my decision to not "be blind." Because I can afford it, I have a plastic surgeon who, on short notice, is available to stitch me up. I need him about once every three months. I'm more or less used to the pain, but it's still a nuisance because of all the time it takes. I'd rather be working or exercising or doing something fun.

If you were to see me in the hallway of my apartment building, you would not realize at first that I am blind. I wear glasses, and my eyes look fairly normal. I even wear a wrist-watch as part of my "costume." But if you had a meal with me, you'd see my hand searching for my water glass and my napkin. Also, I walk slowly, for my own safety. When I meet somebody, I extend my hand first so that other people won't feel embarrassed for me while I search for their hand.

You would think that, after all this time, when I take a walk with my wife and she holds my arm, I wouldn't care what other people think. But I do, a little. I don't like thinking that others are taking pity, imagining how hard our lives are. I don't know if all blind people feel the same way.

People without sight have to trust other people. This can be as simple as trusting a guide to get me where I need to go or trusting a salesperson to give me the correct change, or it can be as complicated as trusting a business partner to read a contract accurately and completely. I have been betrayed a few times in my life, but far more often people have been fair with me. I have learned to make snap decisions about a person's character, and I've gotten pretty good at it.

Sue and I like to go to movies every so often. You might ask, what's the point? Well, I can tell a lot from the dialogue and the music. Also, Sue will whisper what's going on if I need it. An excursion to see a movie is one of the small adventures of a handicapped life, and it means a lot. One time we went to a movie and it was so packed we couldn't sit in the back as we usually do. When Sue started whispering to me, people around us got really annoyed. That gave me stomach cramps, so I had to get up and go to the bathroom, which annoyed people even more. We ended up not going back in. It seems funny now, though at the time it wasn't.

* * *

ONE OF THE STRANGE things about being blind is that people often tell me their secrets, as if they were confessing to a priest. Maybe they think I'm a really good listener (which I am) or that I have special powers (I don't). Other people tend to shy away from me because they're uncomfortable around a blind person. Some of them may think I know things about them they don't want known. Then there are people who ignore me as if I were deaf, mute, and mentally impaired.

Here's another strange thing about blind people: we don't see horizons. Look out the window and you can see where the sky comes down and meets the land. When you look at the ocean, you can see for miles until that flat line where water and sky merge. The horizon is a limit. You might wonder what lies beyond the horizon, but I don't, because for me there is no horizon. In the same way, there are no walls or doors, unless I bump into them. Since I can't see any limits, my imagination is free to go as far as it wants. I think that's one of the reasons I was able to go on from being blind to being a success in my business and personal lives.

When I'm sitting in an unfamiliar room, I know there are hidden dangers, things I could trip over, walls I could run into, and then beyond the door—danger everywhere! But the flip side of having no safe space is that I also see no danger. That may sound odd, but when I sit in a room that has no boundaries (in other words, every room), the only thing out there is the entire universe. It is either completely filled with danger, or it has none at all. It's my choice. And, for the most part, I've chosen not to live in fear.

On balance, then, my life has turned out to have little to do with being blind. On balance, I consider myself the luckiest man in the world. I picked that line up from Lou Gehrig's famous farewell speech at Yankee Stadium on July 4, 1939. He was a great baseball player who died of a terrible disease at age thirty-seven. In that speech, he said, "[For] the past two weeks you have been reading about the bad break I got. Yet today I consider myself the luckiest man on the face of the earth."

So do I.

For Sandy "Glue" Greenberg The toughest, roughest, defender since John Havlicek - Thanks for letting me see the light a few times; my confidence needed it.

Bill Bradley

That's me in the white shirt, "Glue" Greenberg, guarding Bill Bradley—an All-American at Princeton, an all-pro with the New York Knicks, and the former Senator from New Jersey. I can sense the location of the basketball from the flow of people around me.

A Promise

Many blind people are not as lucky as I have been. About 70 percent of blind Americans have no jobs. They do what they can, living off public assistance and their families. It's not an easy life.

Remember that deal I made with God? In the hospital I had vowed to do whatever I could to prevent others from going through the pain of blindness. After I left the White House fellowship, I began thinking more and more about that. I scheduled meetings with businessmen and technology experts to see what efforts were being made to end blindness once and for all.

I started getting people together whenever I could to discuss this and encourage them to continue their work. Science can do amazing things, but it can take years and lots of research, which costs lots of money. The vaccines we now have for any number of diseases were unimaginable a century ago, but scientists kept working and working, solving one problem at a time. One of the people I met with was Dr. Jonas Salk, who was famous for developing a polio vaccine. His encouragement kept me going. And I was still inspired by President Kennedy's moon-shot challenge from the 1960s—an impossibility had become possible because enough people wanted it to happen.

I met with leaders in the field of optic-nerve regeneration. Damage to the optic nerve had been a factor in my own loss of eyesight. If the optic nerve could be repaired, people might regain sight. Another exciting development came along later with the rise of computer technology. Researchers began looking into the possibility of implanting a tiny digital chip into the eyeball to simulate vision.

When I became chairman of the board of governors of the world-famous Johns Hopkins Wilmer Eye Institute in Baltimore, I was in a great position to keep hounding the leading experts to end blindness.

In 2012, my wife and I announced the Sanford and Susan Greenberg Prize—$3 million—to be awarded to researchers in any area of eye disease who are judged to have done the most toward ending blindness. We came up with a target date: 2020.

Sue and I now had a slogan and a goal, "End Blindness 2020." That gave us almost a decade to achieve 20/20—perfect vision. It was crazy, but it helped inspire people.

We presented those awards in December 2020 in a virtual ceremony streamed worldwide. You can watch it, meet the winners, and learn about their amazing progress at endblindnessnow.com.

The September 2016 *National Geographic* cover story, "The End of Blindness," also brought widespread attention to the cause. Now we have launched the Sanford and Susan Greenberg Center to End Blindness as part of the Johns Hopkins University's Wilmer Eye Institute to keep the momentum going and push forward to our final goal: that day when all God's children can not only feel the sun shining on their faces but see its rising and setting with their own two eyes.

The fight continues, in short. Failure is not an option.

* * *

HERE IS A FINAL thought I want to leave with you: We each have a spark of life within us.

A famous prayer in the Jewish religion has taken on new meaning for me. It is the Shehecheyanu: "Blessed art thou, Lord our God, King of the universe, who has kept us in life, sustained us, and enabled us to reach this glorious moment."

I say this prayer every day.

Acknowledgments

No memoir is a solo performance, no matter the teller. Teachers leave their imprint on us, as do rabbis, pastors, priests, coaches, mentors, loved ones, the times we live in and the traditions we inherit. Even if we walk down a road alone, someone else trailblazed the space we travel through.

The blind, though, have a special need for helpers, and for those who have helped me through this life's journey, the word "acknowledgment" seems far too cold. I prefer "gratitude" because I feel it so frequently—gratitude to those who opened up the world to me while I could still see, gratitude to those who led me back to full personhood once my vision had deserted me, maybe most especially gratitude to those who helped me build an adult life not as a person who could not see but as someone who saw in certain ways even more clearly once his sight was gone.

My grandmother Pauline; my mother, Sarah, and fathers, Albert and Carl; Sue and our children, Paul, Jimmy, and Kathryn; my siblings, Joel, Ruth, and Brenda; my college roommates, Art Garfunkel and Jerry Speyer; countless other friends and wise counselors are all part of my sacred litany of blessings. This is a book—and a life—that would not exist without them.

Finally, special thanks to those who have helped turn my narrative into the book in front of you: Publisher Anthony Ziccardi, managing editor Madeline Sturgeon, copy editor Jon Ford, and the entire team at Post Hill Press and Simon & Schuster and my agent, Steve Ross, have been a joy to work with.

Sanford D. Greenberg
Washington, DC

About the Author

Blinded at age nineteen, Sanford D. Greenberg graduated from Columbia University (Phi Beta Kappa) and, following a Marshall Scholarship at Oxford, received his M.A. and Ph.D. at Harvard and M.B.A. at Columbia. He was a White House Fellow under Lyndon B. Johnson and later chaired the federal Rural Healthcare Corporation and served on the National Science Board. His career as an entrepreneur and investor began when he invented, of necessity, a speech-compression machine for those who need to listen and absorb large volumes of printed matter. He subsequently founded several enterprises, including a company that produced specialized computer simulators and the first database tracking antibiotic resistance globally. A Johns Hopkins University and Medicine Trustee Emeritus, Sandy is chairman of the Board of Governors of its Wilmer Eye Institute and founder, along with his wife, Sue, of the Sanford and Susan Greenberg Center to End Blindness at the Johns Hopkins Wilmer Eye Institute, the only facility in the world devoted solely to ending blindness for everyone, forevermore. In a December 2020 ceremony streamed worldwide, Sandy and Sue awarded the initial Greenberg Prizes: $3 million in aggregate to those researchers who have made the greatest progress toward ending blindness for all mankind.

The great artist Frank Stella
created this sculpture,
"Out of Darkness, Light" to
serve as a signpost for our
End Blindness campaign.
Vision Science is a fascinating
field. Maybe you would like
to get involved!